Financial Freedom for Digital Nomads: Mastering Money on the Move

Introduction

Welcome to a comprehensive guide to achieving financial independence and stability tailored specifically for digital nomads and those seeking to navigate the ever-evolving landscape of personal finance. Whether you're a seasoned traveler, a remote worker, or someone simply looking to take control of your financial future, this book offers valuable insights, strategies, and practical advice to help you reach your financial goals.

The Digital Nomad Lifestyle

The digital nomad lifestyle offers unparalleled freedom and flexibility. It allows individuals to work from anywhere in the world, explore new cultures, and create a lifestyle that aligns with their personal values and passions. However, this lifestyle also presents unique financial challenges. Managing money across different currencies, planning for retirement without a traditional employer-sponsored plan, and ensuring financial security while on the move are just a few of the complexities digital nomads face.

Why Financial Independence Matters

Financial independence is more than just a goal; it's a state of financial health that allows you to live life on your terms. It means having the resources and stability to pursue your dreams, support your loved ones, and make choices free from financial constraints. Achieving financial independence requires a blend of strategic planning, disciplined saving and investing, and a proactive approach to managing your finances.

What You'll Learn

This book covers a wide range of topics essential for building a strong financial foundation and navigating the complexities of personal finance. Here's a glimpse of what you'll learn:

- **Foundations of Personal Finance:** Understand the basics of budgeting, saving, investing, and debt management. Learn how to create a solid financial plan tailored to your unique needs.
- **Advanced Investment Strategies:** Dive deep into various investment options, including stocks, bonds, real estate, and cryptocurrencies. Discover how to build a diversified portfolio that aligns with your risk tolerance and financial goals.

- **Retirement Planning:** Explore different retirement planning strategies, including tax-advantaged accounts, social security benefits, and international retirement options. Learn how to create a sustainable retirement plan that ensures long-term financial security.
- **Managing Finances on the Move:** Gain practical tips for managing money as a digital nomad, including currency exchange, banking solutions, and tax considerations. Learn how to maintain financial stability while living a mobile lifestyle.
- **Philanthropy and Social Responsibility:** Understand the importance of giving back and explore ways to integrate philanthropy into your financial plan. Learn about impact investing and how to align your investments with your values.
- **Behavioral Finance and Money Psychology:** Discover the psychological factors that influence financial decision-making. Learn how to overcome cognitive biases, build healthy money habits, and cultivate a positive relationship with money.
- **Utilizing Financial Resources and Tools:** Explore valuable resources, including books, courses, financial advisors, and online communities, to enhance your financial knowledge and support your financial journey.

Our Approach

This book is designed to be both informative and practical. Each chapter provides actionable advice, real-life examples, and step-by-step guidance to help you implement the strategies discussed. We believe that financial education is empowering, and our goal is to equip you with the knowledge and tools you need to take control of your financial future.

We also recognize that personal finance is not a one-size-fits-all endeavor. Your financial journey is unique, shaped by your goals, values, and circumstances. That's why we've included a variety of perspectives and approaches, allowing you to tailor the information to fit your specific needs.

Getting Started

As you embark on this journey towards financial independence and stability, we encourage you to approach it with an open mind and a willingness to learn. Financial success is not achieved overnight; it requires patience, persistence, and continuous growth. Take the time to understand your financial situation, set clear goals, and implement the strategies that resonate with you.

Remember, the path to financial independence is a marathon, not a sprint. There will be challenges along the way, but with the right mindset and the right tools, you can overcome them and build a secure and fulfilling financial future.

Final Thoughts

Thank you for choosing this book as your guide to personal finance. We hope it provides you with valuable insights, practical strategies, and the confidence to take control of your financial future. Whether you're just starting out or looking to refine your financial plan, we're here to support you every step of the way.

Let's embark on this journey together and achieve financial independence, stability, and the freedom to live life on your terms.

The Digital Nomad Lifestyle

The allure of the digital nomad lifestyle is undeniable. With the freedom to work from anywhere in the world, digital nomads can explore new cultures, enjoy diverse experiences, and break free from the constraints of a traditional office job. However, this lifestyle also brings unique financial challenges and opportunities that require careful planning and management.

Introduction to the Digital Nomad Lifestyle

Digital nomads are individuals who leverage technology to perform their jobs remotely, allowing them to travel and live in different locations. This lifestyle has become increasingly popular with the rise of remote work opportunities, advancements in technology, and a growing desire for work-life balance. But while the digital nomad lifestyle offers flexibility and adventure, it also demands a proactive approach to personal finance.

Pros and Cons of Being a Digital Nomad

Like any lifestyle choice, being a digital nomad comes with its own set of advantages and disadvantages.

- **Pros:**
    - Flexibility to work from anywhere
    - Opportunity to travel and experience new cultures
    - Potential for a better work-life balance
    - Increased personal growth and adaptability
- **Cons:**
    - Uncertain and variable income
    - Lack of a stable home base
    - Potential for loneliness and isolation
    - Challenges in managing finances across different countries

Understanding these pros and cons can help aspiring digital nomads make informed decisions about their lifestyle and financial planning.

Financial Implications of a Nomadic Life

Living a nomadic life introduces unique financial considerations. Digital nomads must navigate currency exchange rates, manage international banking, and often deal with fluctuating incomes. Additionally, they need to plan for healthcare, insurance, and retirement in a way that accommodates their mobile lifestyle.

It's essential for digital nomads to develop a flexible financial strategy that allows them to adapt to changing circumstances and locations. This includes building an emergency fund, budgeting for travel expenses, and understanding the financial regulations of different countries.

For instance, digital nomads might face unexpected expenses such as sudden visa changes, medical emergencies, or fluctuating accommodation costs. Having a well-structured financial plan and an emergency fund can provide the necessary cushion to handle these situations without disrupting their lifestyle.

Setting Financial Goals for Digital Nomads

Setting clear financial goals is crucial for digital nomads. These goals can range from short-term objectives like saving for the next trip to long-term plans such as building a retirement fund. By defining these goals, digital nomads can create a roadmap for their financial journey and make informed decisions that support their lifestyle.

Here are some steps to set effective financial goals:

1. **Identify Your Priorities:** Determine what matters most to you, whether it's travel, savings, investments, or debt reduction.
2. **Set Specific Goals:** Make your goals specific, measurable, achievable, relevant, and time-bound (SMART).
3. **Create a Plan:** Develop a detailed plan to achieve your goals, including actionable steps and timelines.
4. **Monitor Progress:** Regularly review your progress and adjust your plan as needed to stay on track.

By following these steps, digital nomads can ensure their financial goals align with their lifestyle and aspirations. For example, if your priority is to travel extensively, you might focus on creating a savings plan that allocates a portion of your income specifically for travel expenses. Alternatively, if building a retirement fund is a priority, you might explore investment opportunities that offer long-term growth.

Creating a Budget: Tracking Income and Expenses

One of the first steps in managing personal finance as a digital nomad is creating a budget. A budget helps track income and expenses, ensuring that you live within your means and save for future goals.

Start by listing all sources of income, including freelance work, remote job salaries, and any passive income streams. Next, categorize your expenses into fixed and variable costs. Fixed costs might include rent, insurance, and loan repayments, while variable costs could include food, entertainment, and travel expenses.

Tracking your expenses is essential to identify areas where you can cut costs and save more. Use financial apps and tools designed for budgeting to simplify this process. Regularly reviewing your budget will help you stay on top of your finances and make necessary adjustments to align with your financial goals.

Building an Emergency Fund

An emergency fund is a critical component of financial stability, especially for digital nomads who might face unpredictable situations. An emergency fund is a savings reserve specifically set aside to cover unexpected expenses such as medical emergencies, travel disruptions, or sudden changes in income.

Aim to save at least three to six months' worth of living expenses in your emergency fund. This fund should be easily accessible, so consider keeping it in a high-yield savings account or a money market account. Building and maintaining an emergency fund will provide peace of mind and financial security, allowing you to focus on enjoying your nomadic lifestyle.

Understanding Currency Exchange and Banking

As a digital nomad, you will frequently deal with multiple currencies and international banking systems. Understanding how to navigate these can save you money and reduce financial stress. Currency exchange rates can fluctuate, impacting your purchasing power and overall budget. It's essential to stay informed about exchange rates and use reliable currency conversion tools.

Consider using international banking solutions that offer multi-currency accounts, low foreign transaction fees, and easy access to your money from anywhere in the world. Digital wallets and fintech solutions can also be beneficial for managing finances across borders. Look for options that provide competitive exchange rates and minimal fees.

Additionally, maintaining financial security is crucial. Ensure that your banking and financial tools offer robust security measures, such as two-factor authentication and encryption, to protect your assets and personal information.

Budgeting and Saving on the Road

One of the most crucial aspects of managing personal finance as a digital nomad is learning how to budget effectively while on the move. A well-structured budget helps ensure that you can maintain your lifestyle, save for future goals, and handle unexpected expenses without stress.

Creating a Flexible Budget

Unlike traditional budgets, a digital nomad's budget needs to be flexible to accommodate varying incomes and expenses. The first step is to identify your sources of income. This may include freelance work, remote job salaries, passive income streams, and any other earnings. Since income can fluctuate, it's essential to estimate your average monthly income based on the past few months.

Next, categorize your expenses into fixed and variable costs. Fixed costs are recurring expenses such as rent, insurance, and loan repayments. Variable costs fluctuate and include food, entertainment, transportation, and travel expenses. Track these expenses diligently using budgeting apps like Mint, YNAB (You Need A Budget), or even a simple spreadsheet.

Allocate a portion of your income to savings, ensuring you set aside funds for both short-term needs and long-term goals. This includes building an emergency fund, saving for future travels, and contributing to retirement accounts.

Managing Variable Income

One of the biggest challenges for digital nomads is managing a variable income. Freelance work and remote jobs often come with irregular pay schedules and fluctuating amounts. To handle this effectively, consider the following strategies:

1. **Buffer Your Budget:** Create a buffer in your budget to cover months when your income is lower than expected. This can be a separate savings account where you set aside surplus income during high-earning months.
2. **Average Your Income:** Calculate your average income over several months and base your budget on this amount. This approach helps smooth out the highs and lows, providing a more stable financial picture.
3. **Track Invoicing and Payments:** Use tools like FreshBooks or QuickBooks to manage invoicing and ensure timely payments. Staying on top of your receivables will help maintain a steady cash flow.

By implementing these strategies, you can manage the uncertainty of variable income and maintain financial stability.

Building an Emergency Fund While Traveling

An emergency fund is a critical component of financial security for digital nomads. It provides a safety net for unexpected expenses such as medical emergencies, travel disruptions, or sudden changes in income. Aim to save at least three to six months' worth of living expenses in your emergency fund.

To build this fund, set aside a portion of your income each month. Consider automating transfers to a high-yield savings account or a money market account. This makes saving consistent and less dependent on manual effort. Regularly review your emergency fund to ensure it keeps pace with your lifestyle and cost of living.

Saving on Travel and Accommodation

As a digital nomad, travel and accommodation are significant expenses. However, there are numerous strategies to save money in these areas:

1. **Use Travel Rewards and Points:** Leverage credit card rewards, frequent flyer miles, and hotel loyalty programs to reduce travel costs. Sign up for cards that offer points for everyday spending and redeem them for flights and accommodation.

2. **Book in Advance:** Planning your travel and accommodation well in advance can result in significant savings. Look for deals on flights, trains, and long-term stays. Websites like Skyscanner, Google Flights, and Airbnb often offer discounts for early bookings.
3. **Opt for Budget-Friendly Accommodation:** Consider alternatives to hotels, such as hostels, house-sitting, and co-living spaces. Websites like Hostelworld, татеHousesitters, and Coliving.com provide affordable options for digital nomads.
4. **Slow Travel:** Staying longer in one location can save money on transportation and accommodation. Many places offer discounts for extended stays, and you can negotiate better rates for long-term rentals.

By adopting these strategies, you can significantly reduce your travel and accommodation expenses, allowing you to allocate more funds to savings and other financial goals.

Tracking Your Expenses

Tracking your expenses is essential for maintaining a healthy budget. It helps you understand where your money is going and identify areas where you can cut back. Use financial tracking apps like Expensify, PocketGuard, or Trail Wallet to monitor your spending. These apps allow you to categorize expenses, set spending limits, and generate reports to visualize your financial habits.

Regularly review your expenses and adjust your budget as needed. This ongoing process ensures that your budget remains realistic and aligned with your financial goals. Additionally, tracking your expenses can help you spot patterns and make more informed decisions about your spending.

Maximizing Savings Through Smart Spending

Smart spending involves making conscious decisions about how you use your money. Here are some tips to maximize your savings through smart spending:

1. **Prioritize Needs Over Wants:** Focus on spending money on necessities and saving on discretionary expenses. This doesn't mean you can't enjoy life, but be mindful of your priorities.
2. **Take Advantage of Discounts and Deals:** Use coupons, cashback apps, and discount websites to save on everyday purchases. Websites like RetailMeNot, Honey, and Rakuten offer deals on a wide range of products and services.
3. **Buy in Bulk:** For items you use regularly, buying in bulk can save money in the long run. This is especially useful for non-perishable goods like toiletries and dry food.
4. **Cook Your Meals:** Eating out frequently can be expensive. Cooking your meals not only saves money but also allows you to eat

healthier. Explore local markets for fresh ingredients and try new recipes. Additionally, cooking can be a fun way to immerse yourself in the local culture.

Implementing these smart spending habits can lead to significant savings, which you can then allocate toward your financial goals.

Leveraging Financial Tools and Apps

In today's digital age, numerous financial tools and apps are available to help digital nomads manage their finances. Here are some recommended tools:

- **Budgeting Apps:** Mint, YNAB, PocketGuard
- **Expense Tracking Apps:** Expensify, Trail Wallet, Money Lover
- **Banking and Transfer Apps:** TransferWise, Revolut, N26
- **Investment Apps:** Robinhood, Acorns, Betterment

These tools can simplify financial management, provide insights into your spending habits, and help you make informed decisions about your money.

Building Wealth through Investing

While budgeting and saving are essential, investing is a powerful way to grow your wealth over time. As a digital nomad, it's crucial to choose investment options that align with your lifestyle and risk tolerance.

Consider a diversified investment portfolio that includes stocks, bonds, mutual funds, and ETFs. If you have a higher risk tolerance, you might explore opportunities in real estate, cryptocurrencies, or peer-to-peer lending. Use investment apps like Robinhood, Acorns, and Betterment to start investing with small amounts of money and gradually build your portfolio.

Regularly review and adjust your investments to ensure they align with your financial goals and market conditions. Staying informed about global economic trends can help you make better investment decisions and maximize your returns.

Retirement Planning for Digital Nomads

Retirement planning is often overlooked by digital nomads, but it's a crucial aspect of financial security. Despite the unconventional lifestyle, digital nomads should prioritize retirement savings to ensure long-term financial stability.

Consider opening and contributing to retirement accounts such as a Roth IRA, Traditional IRA, or Solo 401(k). These accounts offer tax advantages and can be managed from anywhere. Automate your contributions to ensure consistent savings, regardless of income fluctuations.

Additionally, explore international retirement options. Some countries offer favorable conditions for retirees, including lower living costs and tax benefits. Research potential retirement destinations and understand their residency and financial requirements.

Tax Planning and Compliance

Tax planning is a complex but essential aspect of managing finances as a digital nomad. Navigating tax obligations in multiple countries can be challenging, but proper planning can help you minimize tax liability and avoid penalties.

Start by understanding your tax residency status and obligations in your home country and the countries you visit. Some countries have tax treaties that can prevent double taxation, so it's important to know the specifics.

Consider working with an international tax professional who can help you navigate the complexities of tax compliance. They can assist with filing requirements, optimizing deductions, and ensuring you stay compliant with local laws.

Understanding Credit and Debt

As a digital nomad, managing credit and debt effectively is crucial to maintaining financial health. Understanding how credit works, how to build a good credit score, and how to manage debt responsibly can help you achieve financial stability and reach your goals.

The Role of Credit in Personal Finance

Credit plays a significant role in personal finance, allowing you to borrow money for various purposes, such as making large purchases, handling emergencies, or investing in opportunities. Responsible use of credit can help you build a strong credit history, which is essential for securing loans, renting apartments, and even getting better interest rates.

There are different types of credit, including revolving credit (like credit cards) and installment credit (like personal loans or mortgages). Understanding how each type works and how they affect your credit score is essential for managing your finances effectively.

Credit Scores and Reports

Your credit score is a numerical representation of your creditworthiness, based on your credit history. It ranges from 300 to 850, with higher scores indicating better credit. Key factors that influence your credit score include payment history, credit utilization, length of credit history, new credit inquiries, and credit mix.

Regularly monitoring your credit report is important for ensuring accuracy and identifying potential issues. You can obtain a free credit report annually from each of the three major credit bureaus (Equifax, Experian, and TransUnion) through AnnualCreditReport.com. Reviewing your credit report helps you spot errors and detect signs of identity theft early.

Strategies for Building and Maintaining Good Credit

Building and maintaining good credit requires consistent and responsible financial behavior. Here are some strategies to help you achieve and maintain a good credit score:

1. **Pay Your Bills on Time:** Your payment history is the most significant factor in your credit score. Always pay your bills on time to avoid late payments and penalties.

2. **Keep Credit Utilization Low:** Credit utilization is the ratio of your credit card balances to your credit limits. Aim to keep your credit utilization below 30% to positively impact your credit score.
3. **Maintain Long-Term Credit Accounts:** The length of your credit history matters. Keep older accounts open, even if you don't use them frequently, to establish a longer credit history.
4. **Avoid Opening Too Many New Accounts:** Each time you apply for new credit, it results in a hard inquiry, which can temporarily lower your credit score. Avoid opening multiple new accounts in a short period.
5. **Monitor Your Credit Report:** Regularly check your credit report for errors or fraudulent activity. Dispute any inaccuracies with the credit bureaus to keep your credit report accurate.

By following these strategies, you can build and maintain a strong credit profile, which is essential for achieving your financial goals.

Managing Debt Responsibly

Debt management is a critical aspect of personal finance. Whether you have student loans, credit card debt, or personal loans, managing your debt responsibly can help you avoid financial stress and achieve your financial goals. Here are some tips for managing debt effectively:

1. **Create a Debt Repayment Plan:** List all your debts, including balances, interest rates, and minimum payments. Prioritize paying off high-interest debt first while making minimum payments on others.
2. **Consider Debt Consolidation:** If you have multiple high-interest debts, consolidating them into a single loan with a lower interest rate can simplify repayment and reduce overall interest costs.
3. **Avoid Accumulating More Debt:** Be mindful of your spending habits and avoid taking on additional debt while repaying existing debts. Focus on living within your means and budgeting effectively.
4. **Negotiate with Creditors:** If you're struggling to make payments, contact your creditors to discuss alternative payment plans or negotiate lower interest rates. Many creditors are willing to work with you to find a solution.
5. **Seek Professional Help:** If your debt situation is overwhelming, consider seeking help from a credit counseling agency or financial advisor. They can provide guidance and support in creating a debt management plan.

By implementing these strategies, you can manage your debt responsibly and work towards financial freedom.

Avoiding Common Debt Traps

Debt traps can derail your financial progress and lead to long-term financial difficulties. Here are some common debt traps to avoid:

1. **High-Interest Payday Loans:** Payday loans often come with extremely high interest rates and fees. Avoid using payday loans for short-term cash needs and explore alternative options.
2. **Minimum Payment Mentality:** Making only the minimum payment on credit card balances can lead to long-term debt due to accumulating interest. Aim to pay more than the minimum whenever possible.
3. **Unnecessary Large Purchases:** Avoid financing large purchases that are not essential. Save up for such purchases or look for alternatives to reduce debt accumulation.
4. **Ignoring Debt Issues:** Ignoring your debt situation will not make it go away. Face your debt head-on, create a repayment plan, and seek help if needed.

By staying aware of these debt traps and making informed financial decisions, you can avoid falling into debt and maintain financial stability.

Credit and Debt in Different Countries

As a digital nomad, you may encounter different credit systems and debt regulations in various countries. It's essential to understand these differences and adapt your financial strategies accordingly. Here are some key points to consider:

- **Credit Scoring Systems:** Credit scoring systems vary by country. Research how credit scores are calculated in each country you plan to stay in and how to maintain a good credit standing.
- **Local Banking Options:** Different countries have different banking systems and financial products. Explore local banking options that offer favorable terms for digital nomads, such as low fees and convenient access.
- **Currency Exchange and Fees:** Be mindful of currency exchange rates and fees associated with using credit cards and bank accounts internationally. Look for financial products that minimize these costs.
- **Legal Regulations:** Understand the legal regulations regarding debt and credit in each country. This includes knowing your rights as a borrower and any protections available to you.

By understanding the credit and debt landscape in different countries, you can make informed financial decisions and avoid potential pitfalls.

Financial Tools for Managing Credit and Debt

There are several tools and apps available that can help you manage your credit and debt effectively. Here are some recommended options:

- **Credit Monitoring Services:** Services like Credit Karma, Experian, and Equifax provide regular updates on your credit score and report, helping you stay informed about your credit status.
- **Debt Repayment Apps:** Apps like Debt Payoff Planner, Undebt.it, and Tally help you create and manage debt repayment plans, track progress, and stay motivated.
- **Budgeting and Financial Management Apps:** Mint, YNAB, and Personal Capital not only help with budgeting but also provide tools to manage debt and monitor credit.

Using these tools can simplify the process of managing credit and debt, helping you stay on top of your finances and achieve your financial goals.

Real-Life Case Studies

Learning from real-life examples can provide valuable insights into managing credit and debt effectively. Here are a couple of case studies:

Case Study 1: Overcoming High-Interest Debt

Jane, a freelance graphic designer, accumulated significant credit card debt with high interest rates. She decided to tackle her debt by creating a detailed repayment plan. Jane listed all her debts, prioritized paying off the highest-interest debt first, and used the snowball method to stay motivated. She also negotiated with her creditors to lower interest rates and used balance transfer offers to reduce interest costs. Within two years, Jane successfully paid off her debt and significantly improved her credit score.

Case Study 2: Building Credit from Scratch

Tom, a digital nomad from the UK, moved to the US and found that his UK credit history did not transfer. Starting from scratch, Tom opened a secured credit card to begin building his US credit. He used the card responsibly, keeping his credit utilization low and paying his bills on time. Over time, Tom diversified his credit by taking out a small personal loan and gradually increased his credit limit. Within a few years, Tom built a strong US credit profile, enabling him to secure a mortgage for a property investment.

Planning for Future Financial Goals

Effective credit and debt management are crucial for achieving long-term financial goals, such as buying a home, starting a business, or retiring comfortably. Here are some steps to help you plan for your future financial goals:

1. **Set Clear Goals:** Define your short-term and long-term financial goals. Be specific about what you want to achieve and set realistic timelines.
2. **Create a Financial Plan:** Develop a comprehensive financial plan that includes budgeting, saving, investing, and debt management strategies. Use financial tools and apps to help you stay organized and on track.
3. **Regularly Review Your Progress:** Monitor your progress towards your financial goals regularly. Adjust your plan as needed to stay aligned with your objectives and adapt to any changes in your financial situation.
4. **Seek Professional Advice:** Consider working with a financial advisor to help you create and implement a robust financial plan. They can provide personalized advice and support based on your unique circumstances and goals.

By following these steps and managing your credit and debt responsibly, you can work towards achieving your future financial goals and enjoy a secure and fulfilling digital nomad lifestyle.

Smart Investing Principles

Investing is a powerful way to grow your wealth over time and achieve financial independence. For digital nomads, it's essential to understand smart investing principles that align with a mobile lifestyle. This chapter will explore the basics of investing, different types of investments, risk management, and building a diversified investment portfolio.

Introduction to Investing

Investing involves allocating money to assets or ventures with the expectation of generating a profit or income. Unlike saving, which focuses on preserving capital, investing aims to grow your wealth by taking on calculated risks. Understanding the fundamentals of investing is crucial for making informed decisions and achieving long-term financial goals.

The primary goal of investing is to build wealth over time through compound interest, capital appreciation, and income generation. Whether you're investing in stocks, bonds, real estate, or other assets, the key is to start early, invest consistently, and stay informed about market trends and opportunities.

Types of Investments

There are various types of investments, each with its own risk and return characteristics. As a digital nomad, it's important to choose investments that align with your financial goals, risk tolerance, and lifestyle. Here are some common types of investments:

- **Stocks:** Stocks represent ownership in a company. Investing in stocks can provide capital appreciation and dividend income. While stocks can offer high returns, they also come with higher risk and volatility.
- **Bonds:** Bonds are debt securities issued by governments, municipalities, or corporations. They provide regular interest payments and return the principal at maturity. Bonds are generally considered lower-risk investments compared to stocks.
- **Mutual Funds:** Mutual funds pool money from multiple investors to invest in a diversified portfolio of stocks, bonds, or other securities. They offer diversification and professional management but come with management fees.
- **Exchange-Traded Funds (ETFs):** ETFs are similar to mutual funds but trade on stock exchanges like individual stocks. They offer diversification, liquidity, and typically lower fees than mutual funds.
- **Real Estate:** Real estate investments include residential, commercial, and rental properties. Real estate can provide rental income, capital

appreciation, and diversification. However, it requires significant capital and management.
- **Cryptocurrencies:** Cryptocurrencies are digital or virtual currencies that use cryptography for security. Investing in cryptocurrencies can offer high returns but comes with high volatility and regulatory risks.

Diversifying your investments across different asset classes can help spread risk and increase the potential for returns. The right mix of investments depends on your financial goals, risk tolerance, and investment horizon.

Risk Management and Diversification

Risk management is a crucial aspect of investing. While all investments carry some level of risk, understanding and managing these risks can help protect your portfolio and achieve your financial goals. Here are some key risk management strategies:

1. **Diversification:** Diversification involves spreading your investments across different asset classes, sectors, and geographic regions to reduce risk. A diversified portfolio can help mitigate the impact of poor performance in any single investment.
2. **Asset Allocation:** Asset allocation is the process of determining the optimal mix of

asset classes in your portfolio based on your risk tolerance, financial goals, and investment horizon. Regularly review and rebalance your asset allocation to stay aligned with your objectives.
3. **Risk Assessment:** Understand the risk profile of each investment and how it fits into your overall portfolio. Assess factors such as market risk, interest rate risk, inflation risk, and credit risk.
4. **Stop-Loss Orders:** Stop-loss orders are instructions to sell a security when its price reaches a certain level. They can help limit potential losses and protect your investment capital.
5. **Hedging:** Hedging involves using financial instruments, such as options or futures, to offset potential losses in your investments. While hedging can reduce risk, it also comes with costs and complexities.

By implementing these risk management strategies, you can build a resilient investment portfolio that withstands market fluctuations and achieves your long-term financial goals.

Building an Investment Portfolio

Building an investment portfolio involves selecting and managing a collection of investments that align with your financial goals and risk tolerance. Here are the key steps to building a successful investment portfolio:

1. **Define Your Investment Goals:** Identify your short-term and long-term financial goals. Determine the purpose of your investments, whether it's for retirement, buying a home, or achieving financial independence.
2. **Assess Your Risk Tolerance:** Understand your risk tolerance, which is your ability and willingness to take on risk. Consider factors such as your financial situation, investment horizon, and emotional comfort with market volatility.
3. **Determine Your Asset Allocation:** Based on your risk tolerance and investment goals, decide on the optimal mix of asset classes in your portfolio. A common approach is to allocate a percentage of your portfolio to stocks, bonds, and other assets.
4. **Select Your Investments:** Choose individual investments or investment funds that align with your asset allocation strategy. Research and evaluate each investment based on factors such as performance, fees, and risk profile.
5. **Monitor and Rebalance Your Portfolio:** Regularly review your portfolio to ensure it remains aligned with your investment goals and risk tolerance. Rebalance your portfolio by buying or selling investments to maintain your desired asset allocation.
6. **Stay Informed:** Stay informed about market trends, economic developments, and changes in your investments. Continuously educate yourself about investing to make informed

decisions and adapt to changing market conditions.

Building and managing an investment portfolio requires discipline, patience, and a long-term perspective. By following these steps, you can create a diversified portfolio that supports your financial goals and provides growth opportunities.

Investing for Passive Income

As a digital nomad, generating passive income can provide financial stability and freedom. Passive income is earnings derived from investments that require minimal effort to maintain. Here are some popular passive income investments:

- **Dividend Stocks:** Dividend stocks are shares of companies that pay regular dividends to shareholders. Investing in dividend stocks can provide a steady stream of income and potential capital appreciation.
- **Real Estate Investment Trusts (REITs):** REITs are companies that own and operate income-generating real estate. They pay regular dividends to investors and offer a way to invest in real estate without owning physical properties.
- **Peer-to-Peer Lending:** Peer-to-peer lending platforms connect borrowers with individual lenders. Investors earn interest on the loans they fund, generating passive income.

- **Bond Investments:** Bonds provide regular interest payments to investors. While they may offer lower returns than stocks, they are generally less volatile and provide stable income.
- **Index Funds and ETFs:** Index funds and ETFs that focus on dividend-paying stocks or high-yield bonds can provide passive income while offering diversification and professional management.

Investing for passive income can help you achieve financial independence and support your nomadic lifestyle. By diversifying your passive income sources, you can create a reliable income stream that allows you to focus on your passions and adventures.

Tax Considerations for Digital Nomads

As a digital nomad, understanding the tax implications of your investments is crucial for maximizing your returns and staying compliant with tax regulations. Here are some key tax considerations:

- **Tax-Advantaged Accounts:** Take advantage of tax-advantaged accounts such as IRAs, Roth IRAs, and 401(k)s. These accounts offer tax benefits that can help grow your investments more efficiently.
- **Capital Gains Tax:** Understand the capital gains tax rates for your investments. Long-

term capital gains (investments held for more than a year) are typically taxed at lower rates than short-term capital gains.
- **Foreign Tax Credits:** If you earn investment income in foreign countries, you may be eligible for foreign tax credits. These credits can help offset taxes paid to other countries, reducing your overall tax liability.
- **Double Taxation Agreements:** Research double taxation agreements between your home country and the countries you reside in. These agreements can prevent double taxation on your investment income.
- **Reporting Requirements:** Stay informed about the reporting requirements for your investments, including foreign assets and accounts. Failure to comply with reporting obligations can result in penalties and fines.

Consulting with a tax professional who specializes in international tax can help you navigate the complexities of tax planning and ensure you optimize your tax strategy for your investments.

Real Estate and Property Investment

Real estate and property investment can be an excellent way to diversify your portfolio, generate passive income, and achieve long-term financial growth. For digital nomads, investing in real estate requires careful planning and consideration of various factors unique to their lifestyle. This chapter will explore different types of real estate investments, strategies for buying and managing properties, and tips for leveraging real estate to build wealth.

Introduction to Real Estate Investment

Real estate investment involves purchasing, owning, managing, and selling properties for profit. Unlike stocks and bonds, real estate is a tangible asset that can provide a steady income stream and potential capital appreciation. Real estate investments can include residential properties, commercial properties, rental properties, and real estate investment trusts (REITs).

For digital nomads, real estate can offer a stable income source through rental properties and diversification of their investment portfolio. However, real estate investment also comes with challenges such as property management, market fluctuations, and liquidity issues. Understanding these factors and developing a strategic approach is crucial for success.

Types of Real Estate Investments

There are various types of real estate investments, each with its own characteristics and benefits. Here are some common types of real estate investments:

- **Residential Properties:** Residential real estate includes single-family homes, condominiums, townhouses, and multi-family properties. Investing in residential properties can provide rental income and potential appreciation.
- **Commercial Properties:** Commercial real estate includes office buildings, retail spaces, warehouses, and industrial properties. These properties can offer higher rental income and longer lease terms but may require more substantial capital investment.
- **Rental Properties:** Rental properties are residential or commercial properties that generate rental income. They can provide a steady cash flow and potential tax benefits but require active management and maintenance.
- **Real Estate Investment Trusts (REITs):** REITs are companies that own and operate income-generating real estate. They offer a way to invest in real estate without owning physical properties and provide liquidity, diversification, and regular dividends.

- **Vacation Rentals:** Vacation rentals, such as Airbnb properties, can provide high rental income during peak seasons. However, they require active management, marketing, and compliance with local regulations.

Each type of real estate investment has its own risk and return profile. It's important to assess your financial goals, risk tolerance, and investment horizon when choosing the right type of real estate investment for your portfolio.

Buying Your First Property

Buying your first property is a significant milestone in real estate investment. As a digital nomad, it's essential to consider factors such as location, financing, and property management. Here are some steps to guide you through the process:

1. **Set Your Investment Goals:** Define your objectives for investing in real estate. Are you looking for rental income, long-term appreciation, or a vacation home that you can rent out when not in use?
2. **Research Locations:** Location is a critical factor in real estate investment. Research areas with strong rental demand, potential for appreciation, and favorable market conditions. Consider factors such as job growth, population trends, and local amenities.
3. **Secure Financing:** Explore financing options such as mortgages, private loans, or

partnerships. As a digital nomad, it may be challenging to secure traditional financing, so consider alternative lenders or strategies such as owner financing.
4. **Conduct Due Diligence:** Perform thorough due diligence on the property, including inspections, title searches, and market analysis. Ensure the property is in good condition and free of legal issues.
5. **Negotiate and Close the Deal:** Negotiate the purchase price and terms with the seller. Work with a real estate attorney or agent to navigate the closing process and ensure all legal and financial aspects are handled properly.

Buying your first property requires careful planning and research. By following these steps, you can make informed decisions and set the foundation for a successful real estate investment.

Managing Rental Properties

Managing rental properties can be both rewarding and challenging. Effective property management ensures a steady rental income, satisfied tenants, and well-maintained properties. Here are some tips for managing rental properties as a digital nomad:

1. **Hire a Property Manager:** Consider hiring a professional property manager to handle day-to-day operations, tenant interactions, and maintenance. A property manager can save you time and provide local expertise,

especially if you invest in properties located far from your current location.
2. **Use Property Management Software:** Utilize property management software to streamline tasks such as rent collection, maintenance requests, and tenant communication. Software solutions like Buildium, AppFolio, and TenantCloud can help you manage your properties remotely.
3. **Screen Tenants Carefully:** Conduct thorough tenant screenings to ensure you select reliable and responsible tenants. Check their credit history, rental references, and employment status to minimize the risk of late payments and property damage.
4. **Establish Clear Lease Agreements:** Draft comprehensive lease agreements that outline tenant responsibilities, rent payment terms, and property rules. Clear agreements help prevent disputes and ensure a smooth landlord-tenant relationship.
5. **Maintain Regular Communication:** Stay in regular contact with your tenants to address any concerns promptly and build positive relationships. Effective communication can lead to longer tenancies and fewer vacancies.
6. **Plan for Maintenance and Repairs:** Set aside a portion of your rental income for maintenance and repairs. Regularly inspect your properties and address issues promptly to maintain their value and appeal.

Managing rental properties requires a proactive approach and attention to detail. By implementing these strategies, you can effectively manage your properties and maximize your rental income.

Real Estate Investment Strategies

There are various real estate investment strategies that can help you achieve your financial goals. Here are some popular strategies:

- **Buy and Hold:** This strategy involves purchasing properties to hold for the long term, generating rental income and benefiting from property appreciation. It's a common strategy for building wealth over time.
- **Fix and Flip:** Fix and flip involves buying distressed properties, renovating them, and selling them for a profit. This strategy requires a good understanding of the real estate market, renovation costs, and project management.
- **Short-Term Rentals:** Investing in vacation rentals or Airbnb properties can provide high rental income, especially in popular tourist destinations. However, it requires active management and compliance with local regulations.
- **Real Estate Crowdfunding:** Real estate crowdfunding platforms allow you to invest in real estate projects with a relatively small amount of capital. It's a way to diversify your real estate investments without owning physical properties.
- **House Hacking:** House hacking involves living in one unit of a multi-family property

while renting out the other units to cover your mortgage and expenses. It's an effective way to reduce housing costs and build equity.

Each real estate investment strategy has its own risk and return profile. Choose the strategy that aligns with your financial goals, risk tolerance, and available resources.

Leveraging Real Estate to Build Wealth

Real estate can be a powerful tool for building wealth and achieving financial independence. Here are some ways to leverage real estate to build wealth:

1. **Generate Passive Income:** Rental properties can provide a steady stream of passive income, allowing you to cover expenses and reinvest in additional properties.
2. **Benefit from Appreciation:** Real estate properties tend to appreciate over time, increasing your net worth. Choose properties in areas with strong growth potential to maximize appreciation.
3. **Utilize Tax Benefits:** Real estate investments offer various tax benefits, including deductions for mortgage interest, property taxes, depreciation, and operating expenses. Consult with a tax professional to optimize your tax strategy.
4. **Leverage Financing:** Using leverage, or borrowed capital, allows you to control larger

assets with a smaller investment. While leverage can amplify returns, it also increases risk, so use it wisely.
5. **Build Equity:** As you pay down your mortgage, you build equity in your property. This equity can be used to secure additional financing or as a safety net for future investments.

By leveraging real estate strategically, you can build a diversified portfolio that generates income, appreciates in value, and provides financial security.

Case Studies and Success Stories

Learning from real-life examples can provide valuable insights into successful real estate investment strategies. Here are a couple of case studies:

Case Study 1: From Rental Property to Real Estate Empire

Emily, a digital nomad and freelance writer, started her real estate journey by purchasing a small rental property in her hometown. With a keen eye for undervalued properties and a knack for property management, Emily quickly turned her first investment into a profitable venture. She reinvested the rental income into additional properties, leveraging financing options to expand her portfolio. Today, Emily owns a diverse range of rental properties across multiple states, generating significant passive income that supports her nomadic lifestyle.

Case Study 2: Vacation Rentals for High Seasonal Income

James, an IT consultant and avid traveler, saw an opportunity in the booming vacation rental market. He purchased a beachfront property in a popular tourist destination and transformed it into a luxurious vacation rental. By leveraging platforms like Airbnb and VRBO, James attracted high-paying guests during peak seasons. The rental income not only covered his mortgage but also provided a substantial profit. Encouraged by his success, James invested in additional vacation properties in other tourist hotspots, creating a network of high-income vacation rentals.

Navigating Legal and Regulatory Challenges

Real estate investment involves navigating various legal and regulatory challenges, especially as a digital nomad. Here are some key considerations:

- **Local Laws and Regulations:** Understand the local laws and regulations governing real estate investment in the areas you invest. This includes zoning laws, rental regulations, and property tax requirements.

- **Compliance with Housing Codes:** Ensure your properties comply with local housing codes and safety standards. Regular inspections and maintenance can help you stay compliant and avoid legal issues.
- **Tenant Rights and Landlord Responsibilities:** Familiarize yourself with tenant rights and landlord responsibilities in each location. Clear lease agreements and transparent communication can help prevent disputes and legal complications.
- **Short-Term Rental Regulations:** Many cities have specific regulations for short-term rentals. Ensure you comply with licensing, tax collection, and occupancy limits to avoid fines and legal issues.
- **Insurance Coverage:** Obtain adequate insurance coverage for your properties, including liability, property, and rental income insurance. Proper insurance can protect you from financial losses and legal liabilities.

By staying informed and proactive about legal and regulatory challenges, you can protect your real estate investments and ensure long-term success.

Retirement Planning on the Move

Retirement planning is a crucial aspect of financial management for everyone, including digital nomads. Despite the unconventional lifestyle, it's essential to prepare for a secure and comfortable retirement. This chapter will explore the importance of retirement planning, different types of retirement accounts, strategies for saving and investing, and considerations for retiring abroad.

The Importance of Early Retirement Planning

Starting your retirement planning early can significantly impact your financial security in the future. The power of compound interest means that the earlier you start saving and investing, the more your money can grow over time. Early planning also allows you to take advantage of tax-deferred growth and employer contributions, where applicable.

For digital nomads, early retirement planning is especially important due to potential fluctuations in income and the need for a flexible approach to saving and investing. By starting early, you can build a substantial retirement fund that supports your desired lifestyle in your later years.

Types of Retirement Accounts

There are various types of retirement accounts, each with its own tax advantages and contribution limits. Understanding these options can help you choose the best accounts for your retirement savings. Here are some common types of retirement accounts:

- **401(k) Plans:** Employer-sponsored retirement plans that allow you to contribute a portion of your salary on a pre-tax basis. Many employers offer matching contributions, which can significantly boost your retirement savings.
- **Traditional IRA:** Individual Retirement Accounts (IRAs) that allow you to contribute pre-tax income, with investments growing tax-deferred until withdrawal. Withdrawals are taxed as ordinary income in retirement.
- **Roth IRA:** IRAs funded with after-tax income, with qualified withdrawals being tax-free in retirement. Roth IRAs are beneficial if you expect to be in a higher tax bracket in retirement.
- **Solo 401(k):** A retirement plan for self-employed individuals or small business owners with no full-time employees. It offers high contribution limits and tax advantages similar to traditional 401(k) plans.
- **SEP IRA:** Simplified Employee Pension IRAs are designed for self-employed individuals and small business owners. They

allow for substantial contributions and offer tax-deferred growth.

Choosing the right retirement accounts depends on your employment status, income level, and tax situation. Diversifying your retirement savings across different accounts can provide flexibility and maximize tax benefits.

Strategies for Building a Retirement Nest Egg

Building a substantial retirement nest egg requires a combination of saving, investing, and strategic planning. Here are some strategies to help you achieve your retirement goals:

1. **Maximize Contributions:** Take full advantage of the contribution limits for your retirement accounts. If your employer offers a matching contribution, aim to contribute at least enough to receive the full match.
2. **Automate Savings:** Set up automatic contributions to your retirement accounts to ensure consistent saving. Automating your savings helps you stay disciplined and avoid the temptation to spend instead.
3. **Diversify Investments:** Diversify your retirement investments across different asset classes, such as stocks, bonds, and real estate. Diversification can help manage risk and improve potential returns.

4. **Rebalance Regularly:** Regularly review and rebalance your investment portfolio to maintain your desired asset allocation. Rebalancing ensures that your portfolio stays aligned with your risk tolerance and financial goals.
5. **Consider Tax Efficiency:** Be mindful of the tax implications of your investments. Utilize tax-advantaged accounts and strategies to minimize your tax liability and maximize your after-tax returns.
6. **Plan for Healthcare Costs:** Healthcare can be a significant expense in retirement. Consider contributing to a Health Savings Account (HSA) if eligible, as HSAs offer tax advantages and can be used for medical expenses in retirement.

By implementing these strategies, you can build a robust retirement nest egg that provides financial security and peace of mind.

Retirement Options in Different Countries

Retiring abroad can offer exciting opportunities and potential cost savings. However, it's essential to understand the financial and legal implications of retiring in a different country. Here are some key considerations:

- **Cost of Living:** Research the cost of living in your desired retirement destination. Some countries offer a lower cost of living, which can stretch your retirement savings further.
- **Healthcare:** Investigate the quality and cost of healthcare in the country. Ensure you have adequate health insurance coverage, either through local insurance plans or international health insurance.
- **Visa and Residency Requirements:** Understand the visa and residency requirements for retirees. Some countries offer retirement visas with specific financial requirements and benefits.
- **Tax Implications:** Consider the tax implications of retiring abroad, including how your retirement income will be taxed. Research any tax treaties between your home country and your retirement destination to avoid double taxation.
- **Currency Exchange and Banking:** Be mindful of currency exchange rates and banking options. Having a local bank account can simplify financial transactions and reduce currency exchange fees.
- **Legal Considerations:** Understand the legal aspects of property ownership, inheritance laws, and estate planning in your chosen country. Consulting with a local attorney can help you navigate these complexities.

Retiring abroad requires careful planning and research, but it can offer a fulfilling and financially advantageous lifestyle. Consider visiting potential retirement destinations to get a firsthand experience before making your decision.

Case Studies and Success Stories

Learning from real-life examples can provide valuable insights into successful retirement planning for digital nomads. Here are a couple of case studies:

Case Study 1: Retiring in a Low-Cost Country

Lisa, a freelance graphic designer, spent her career working remotely and traveling the world. As she approached retirement, Lisa decided to settle in Thailand, attracted by its affordable cost of living and vibrant culture. By thoroughly researching visa options, healthcare, and the local property market, Lisa secured a comfortable apartment and set up a local bank account. Her retirement savings stretched further in Thailand, allowing her to live a comfortable and fulfilling retirement lifestyle.

Case Study 2: Diversifying Retirement Investments

John, a software developer, knew the importance of early retirement planning. Throughout his career, he contributed to a 401(k) plan, a Roth IRA, and invested in real estate properties. John diversified his investments across stocks, bonds, and rental properties, providing multiple income streams in retirement. As a digital nomad, John leveraged online financial tools to manage his investments and monitor his progress. His strategic approach to retirement planning allowed him to retire comfortably and continue exploring the world.

Planning for a Flexible Retirement

Flexibility is a key consideration for digital nomads planning their retirement. Here are some tips for creating a flexible retirement plan:

1. **Maintain Multiple Income Streams:** Diversify your retirement income sources, including pensions, Social Security, investments, and rental income. Multiple income streams provide financial stability and flexibility.
2. **Stay Mobile:** Consider maintaining a flexible living arrangement, such as renting or owning property in multiple locations. This allows you to move easily and adapt to changing circumstances.
3. **Continue Working Part-Time:** If desired, consider part-time or freelance work in retirement. Continuing to work can provide additional income, keep you engaged, and offer a sense of purpose.
4. **Stay Informed:** Keep up with changes in tax laws, healthcare, and retirement regulations

that may affect your retirement plan. Staying informed helps you adapt your plan as needed.
5. **Maintain a Healthy Lifestyle:** A healthy lifestyle can significantly impact your quality of life in retirement. Focus on maintaining physical and mental health through regular exercise, a balanced diet, and engaging in social and recreational activities.

By planning for flexibility, you can enjoy a dynamic and fulfilling retirement that aligns with your adventurous spirit.

Tax Strategies for Retirement

Effective tax planning can help maximize your retirement income and minimize tax liabilities. Here are some tax strategies to consider for retirement:

1. **Roth Conversions:** Converting a portion of your traditional IRA or 401(k) to a Roth IRA can provide tax-free withdrawals in retirement. Consider doing this in years when your income is lower to minimize the tax impact of the conversion.
2. **Utilize Tax-Deferred Accounts:** Continue contributing to tax-deferred retirement accounts like traditional IRAs and 401(k)s to reduce your taxable income during your working years. Withdrawals will be taxed in retirement, but you may be in a lower tax bracket.

3. **Take Advantage of Standard Deductions:** Plan your withdrawals and income to take full advantage of standard deductions and personal exemptions, minimizing your taxable income.
4. **Consider Charitable Giving:** Donating appreciated assets or making Qualified Charitable Distributions (QCDs) from your IRA can reduce your taxable income while supporting charitable causes.
5. **Strategize Social Security Benefits:** Plan the timing of your Social Security benefits to maximize your lifetime benefits and minimize taxes. Delaying benefits can increase your monthly payout and potentially reduce the portion of benefits subject to tax.

Consulting with a tax professional who specializes in retirement planning can help you implement these strategies effectively and optimize your tax situation in retirement.

Healthcare Planning for Retirement

Healthcare is a significant concern for retirees, and planning for healthcare expenses is essential for financial security. Here are some tips for healthcare planning in retirement:

1. **Understand Medicare:** Familiarize yourself with Medicare coverage options, including Parts A, B, C, and D. Understand the costs,

coverage, and enrollment periods to make informed decisions about your healthcare.
2. **Consider Supplemental Insurance:** Medicare may not cover all healthcare expenses. Consider purchasing supplemental insurance (Medigap) or a Medicare Advantage plan to cover additional costs such as copayments, deductibles, and prescription drugs.
3. **Plan for Long-Term Care:** Long-term care can be a significant expense in retirement. Consider long-term care insurance or alternative strategies to cover potential costs, such as creating a dedicated savings fund or utilizing home equity.
4. **Maintain a Healthy Lifestyle:** Investing in your health through regular exercise, a balanced diet, and preventive care can help reduce healthcare costs and improve your quality of life in retirement.
5. **Explore International Health Insurance:** If you plan to retire abroad, research international health insurance options that provide coverage in your chosen country. Ensure the insurance includes emergency medical evacuation and repatriation benefits.

Proactive healthcare planning can help you manage healthcare costs and ensure you have access to quality care throughout your retirement.

Creating a Retirement Withdrawal Strategy

A well-planned withdrawal strategy is essential for ensuring your retirement savings last throughout your lifetime. Here are some tips for creating an effective withdrawal strategy:

1. **Determine Your Withdrawal Rate:** A common rule of thumb is the 4% rule, which suggests withdrawing 4% of your retirement savings annually. Adjust this rate based on your individual needs, risk tolerance, and life expectancy.
2. **Sequence of Withdrawals:** Plan the order in which you withdraw funds from your accounts. Consider withdrawing from taxable accounts first, then tax-deferred accounts, and finally tax-free accounts like Roth IRAs to optimize tax efficiency.
3. **Adjust for Market Conditions:** Be flexible with your withdrawal strategy and adjust your withdrawals based on market performance. In years of poor market performance, consider reducing withdrawals to preserve your portfolio.
4. **Include Guaranteed Income Sources:** Incorporate guaranteed income sources such as Social Security, pensions, and annuities into your withdrawal strategy to provide a stable income foundation.

5. **Regularly Review Your Strategy:** Regularly review and adjust your withdrawal strategy based on changes in your financial situation, life expectancy, and market conditions. Consulting with a financial advisor can help you stay on track and make informed decisions.

Creating a flexible and sustainable withdrawal strategy ensures that your retirement savings last and provides financial security throughout your retirement.

Retirement planning is essential for ensuring a secure and comfortable future. For digital nomads, planning for retirement requires careful consideration of unique challenges and opportunities. This chapter will explore strategies for saving, investing, and planning for retirement while maintaining a mobile lifestyle.

The Importance of Early Retirement Planning

Starting your retirement planning early can significantly impact your financial security in the future. The power of compound interest means that the earlier you start saving and investing, the more your money can grow over time. Early planning also allows you to take advantage of tax-deferred growth and employer contributions, where applicable.

For digital nomads, early retirement planning is especially important due to potential fluctuations in income and the need for a flexible approach to saving and investing. By starting early, you can build a substantial retirement fund that supports your desired lifestyle in your later years.

Types of Retirement Accounts

There are various types of retirement accounts, each with its own tax advantages and contribution limits. Understanding these options can help you choose the best accounts for your retirement savings. Here are some common types of retirement accounts:

- **401(k) Plans:** Employer-sponsored retirement plans that allow you to contribute a portion of your salary on a pre-tax basis. Many employers offer matching contributions, which can significantly boost your retirement savings.
- **Traditional IRA:** Individual Retirement Accounts (IRAs) that allow you to contribute pre-tax income, with investments growing tax-deferred until withdrawal. Withdrawals are taxed as ordinary income in retirement.
- **Roth IRA:** IRAs funded with after-tax income, with qualified withdrawals being tax-free in retirement. Roth IRAs are beneficial if you expect to be in a higher tax bracket in retirement.
- **Solo 401(k):** A retirement plan for self-employed individuals or small business owners with no full-time employees. It offers

high contribution limits and tax advantages similar to traditional 401(k) plans.
- **SEP IRA:** Simplified Employee Pension IRAs are designed for self-employed individuals and small business owners. They allow for substantial contributions and offer tax-deferred growth.

Choosing the right retirement accounts depends on your employment status, income level, and tax situation. Diversifying your retirement savings across different accounts can provide flexibility and maximize tax benefits.

Strategies for Building a Retirement Nest Egg

Building a substantial retirement nest egg requires a combination of saving, investing, and strategic planning. Here are some strategies to help you achieve your retirement goals:

1. **Maximize Contributions:** Take full advantage of the contribution limits for your retirement accounts. If your employer offers a matching contribution, aim to contribute at least enough to receive the full match.
2. **Automate Savings:** Set up automatic contributions to your retirement accounts to ensure consistent saving. Automating your savings helps you stay disciplined and avoid the temptation to spend instead.

3. **Diversify Investments:** Diversify your retirement investments across different asset classes, such as stocks, bonds, and real estate. Diversification can help manage risk and improve potential returns.
4. **Rebalance Regularly:** Regularly review and rebalance your investment portfolio to maintain your desired asset allocation. Rebalancing ensures that your portfolio stays aligned with your risk tolerance and financial goals.
5. **Consider Tax Efficiency:** Be mindful of the tax implications of your investments. Utilize tax-advantaged accounts and strategies to minimize your tax liability and maximize your after-tax returns.
6. **Plan for Healthcare Costs:** Healthcare can be a significant expense in retirement. Consider contributing to a Health Savings Account (HSA) if eligible, as HSAs offer tax advantages and can be used for medical expenses in retirement.

By implementing these strategies, you can build a robust retirement nest egg that provides financial security and peace of mind.

Retirement Options in Different Countries

Retiring abroad can offer exciting opportunities and potential cost savings. However, it's essential to understand the financial and legal implications of retiring in a different country. Here are some key considerations:

- **Cost of Living:** Research the cost of living in your desired retirement destination. Some countries offer a lower cost of living, which can stretch your retirement savings further.
- **Healthcare:** Investigate the quality and cost of healthcare in the country. Ensure you have adequate health insurance coverage, either through local insurance plans or international health insurance.
- **Visa and Residency Requirements:** Understand the visa and residency requirements for retirees. Some countries offer retirement visas with specific financial requirements and benefits.
- **Tax Implications:** Consider the tax implications of retiring abroad, including how your retirement income will be taxed. Research any tax treaties between your home country and your retirement destination to avoid double taxation.
- **Currency Exchange and Banking:** Be mindful of currency exchange rates and banking options. Having a local bank account can simplify financial transactions and reduce currency exchange fees.
- **Legal Considerations:** Understand the legal aspects of property ownership, inheritance laws, and estate planning in your chosen

country. Consulting with a local attorney can help you navigate these complexities.

Retiring abroad requires careful planning and research, but it can offer a fulfilling and financially advantageous lifestyle. Consider visiting potential retirement destinations to get a firsthand experience before making your decision.

Case Studies and Success Stories

Learning from real-life examples can provide valuable insights into successful retirement planning for digital nomads. Here are a couple of case studies:

Case Study 1: Retiring in a Low-Cost Country

Lisa, a freelance graphic designer, spent her career working remotely and traveling the world. As she approached retirement, Lisa decided to settle in Thailand, attracted by its affordable cost of living and vibrant culture. By thoroughly researching visa options, healthcare, and the local property market, Lisa secured a comfortable apartment and set up a local bank account. Her retirement savings stretched further in Thailand, allowing her to live a comfortable and fulfilling retirement lifestyle.

Case Study 2: Diversifying Retirement Investments

John, a software developer, knew the importance of early retirement planning. Throughout his career, he contributed to a 401(k) plan, a Roth IRA, and invested in real estate properties. John diversified his investments across stocks, bonds, and rental properties, providing multiple income streams in retirement. As a digital nomad, John leveraged online financial tools to manage his investments and monitor his progress. His strategic approach to retirement planning allowed him to retire comfortably and continue exploring the world.

Planning for a Flexible Retirement

Flexibility is a key consideration for digital nomads planning their retirement. Here are some tips for creating a flexible retirement plan:

1. **Maintain Multiple Income Streams:** Diversify your retirement income sources, including pensions, Social Security, investments, and rental income. Multiple income streams provide financial stability and flexibility.
2. **Stay Mobile:** Consider maintaining a flexible living arrangement, such as renting or owning property in multiple locations. This allows

you to move easily and adapt to changing circumstances.
3. **Continue Working Part-Time:** If desired, consider part-time or freelance work in retirement. Continuing to work can provide additional income, keep you engaged, and offer a sense of purpose.
4. **Stay Informed:** Keep up with changes in tax laws, healthcare, and retirement regulations that may affect your retirement plan. Staying informed helps you adapt your plan as needed.
5. **Maintain a Healthy Lifestyle:** A healthy lifestyle can significantly impact your quality of life in retirement. Focus on maintaining physical and mental health through regular exercise, a balanced diet, and engaging in social and recreational activities.

By planning for flexibility, you can enjoy a dynamic and fulfilling retirement that aligns with your adventurous spirit.

Tax Strategies for Retirement

Effective tax planning can help maximize your retirement income and minimize tax liabilities. Here are some tax strategies to consider for retirement:

1. **Roth Conversions:** Converting a portion of your traditional IRA or 401(k) to a Roth IRA can provide tax-free withdrawals in retirement. Consider doing this in years when

your income is lower to minimize the tax impact of the conversion.
2. **Utilize Tax-Deferred Accounts:** Continue contributing to tax-deferred retirement accounts like traditional IRAs and 401(k)s to reduce your taxable income during your working years. Withdrawals will be taxed in retirement, but you may be in a lower tax bracket.
3. **Take Advantage of Standard Deductions:** Plan your withdrawals and income to take full advantage of standard deductions and personal exemptions, minimizing your taxable income.
4. **Consider Charitable Giving:** Donating appreciated assets or making Qualified Charitable Distributions (QCDs) from your IRA can reduce your taxable income while supporting charitable causes.
5. **Strategize Social Security Benefits:** Plan the timing of your Social Security benefits to maximize your lifetime benefits and minimize taxes. Delaying benefits can increase your monthly payout and potentially reduce the portion of benefits subject to tax.

Consulting with a tax professional who specializes in retirement planning can help you implement these strategies effectively and optimize your tax situation in retirement.

Healthcare Planning for Retirement

Healthcare is a significant concern for retirees, and planning for healthcare expenses is essential for financial security. Here are some tips for healthcare planning in retirement:

1. **Understand Medicare:** Familiarize yourself with Medicare coverage options, including Parts A, B, C, and D. Understand the costs, coverage, and enrollment periods to make informed decisions about your healthcare.
2. **Consider Supplemental Insurance:** Medicare may not cover all healthcare expenses. Consider purchasing supplemental insurance (Medigap) or a Medicare Advantage plan to cover additional costs such as copayments, deductibles, and prescription drugs.
3. **Plan for Long-Term Care:** Long-term care can be a significant expense in retirement. Consider long-term care insurance or alternative strategies to cover potential costs, such as creating a dedicated savings fund or utilizing home equity.
4. **Maintain a Healthy Lifestyle:** Investing in your health through regular exercise, a balanced diet, and preventive care can help reduce healthcare costs and improve your quality of life in retirement.

5. **Explore International Health Insurance:** If you plan to retire abroad, research international health insurance options that provide coverage in your chosen country. Ensure the insurance includes emergency medical evacuation and repatriation benefits.

Proactive healthcare planning can help you manage healthcare costs and ensure you have access to quality care throughout your retirement.

Creating a Retirement Withdrawal Strategy

A well-planned withdrawal strategy is essential for ensuring your retirement savings last throughout your lifetime. Here are some tips for creating an effective withdrawal strategy:

1. **Determine Your Withdrawal Rate:** A common rule of thumb is the 4% rule, which suggests withdrawing 4% of your retirement savings annually. Adjust this rate based on your individual needs, risk tolerance, and life expectancy.
2. **Sequence of Withdrawals:** Plan the order in which you withdraw funds from your accounts. Consider withdrawing from taxable accounts first, then tax-deferred accounts, and finally tax-free accounts like Roth IRAs to optimize tax efficiency.
3. **Adjust for Market Conditions:** Be flexible with your withdrawal strategy and adjust your

withdrawals based on market performance. In years of poor market performance, consider reducing withdrawals to preserve your portfolio.
4. **Include Guaranteed Income Sources:** Incorporate guaranteed income sources such as Social Security, pensions, and annuities into your withdrawal strategy to provide a stable income foundation.
5. **Regularly Review Your Strategy:** Regularly review and adjust your withdrawal strategy based on changes in your financial situation, life expectancy, and market conditions. Consulting with a financial advisor can help you stay on track and make informed decisions.

Creating a flexible and sustainable withdrawal strategy ensures that your retirement savings last and provides financial security throughout your retirement.

Tax Planning and Compliance

Tax planning is a critical aspect of financial management for digital nomads. Navigating tax obligations in multiple countries can be complex, but proper planning can help you minimize tax liability and avoid penalties. This chapter will explore the basics of tax planning, strategies for reducing taxes, and tips for staying compliant with tax regulations.

Understanding Tax Residency

One of the first steps in tax planning for digital nomads is understanding tax residency. Tax residency determines where you are liable to pay taxes. Each country has its own rules for determining tax residency, which can be based on physical presence, domicile, or other factors.

For example, in the United States, you are considered a tax resident if you meet the substantial presence test or hold a Green Card. Many other countries use a similar system based on the number of days you spend in the country. It's essential to research the tax residency rules of the countries you live in and ensure you comply with their requirements.

Double Taxation and Tax Treaties

Double taxation occurs when you are taxed on the same income in two different countries. To avoid this, many countries have double taxation agreements (DTAs) or tax treaties in place. These treaties outline which country has the right to tax specific types of income and provide methods to eliminate or reduce double taxation.

For digital nomads, it's crucial to understand the tax treaties between your home country and the countries where you reside or earn income. Utilizing tax treaties can help you avoid paying taxes twice on the same income and reduce your overall tax burden.

Foreign Earned Income Exclusion (FEIE)

The Foreign Earned Income Exclusion (FEIE) is a provision that allows U.S. citizens and resident aliens living abroad to exclude a certain amount of foreign-earned income from their taxable income. For 2023, the exclusion amount is up to $112,000.

To qualify for the FEIE, you must meet either the bona fide residence test or the physical presence test:

- **Bona Fide Residence Test:** You must be a bona fide resident of a foreign country for an

uninterrupted period that includes an entire tax year.
- **Physical Presence Test:** You must be physically present in a foreign country or countries for at least 330 full days during a 12-month period.

Utilizing the FEIE can significantly reduce your U.S. tax liability, but it's essential to keep accurate records and file the necessary forms with your tax return.

Foreign Tax Credit (FTC)

The Foreign Tax Credit (FTC) is another provision that helps U.S. taxpayers avoid double taxation. The FTC allows you to claim a credit for foreign income taxes paid or accrued during the tax year. This credit can be applied against your U.S. tax liability on the same income.

To claim the FTC, you must complete Form 1116 and include it with your U.S. tax return. It's essential to keep detailed records of foreign taxes paid and ensure you do not claim both the FEIE and FTC on the same income.

Tax-Advantaged Accounts

Contributing to tax-advantaged accounts can help reduce your taxable income and grow your savings more efficiently. Here are some common tax-advantaged accounts:

- **Traditional IRA:** Contributions to a traditional IRA are tax-deductible, and investments grow tax-deferred until withdrawal. Withdrawals are taxed as ordinary income in retirement.
- **Roth IRA:** Contributions to a Roth IRA are made with after-tax income, but qualified withdrawals are tax-free in retirement.
- **401(k):** Employer-sponsored retirement plans that allow you to contribute pre-tax income. Many employers offer matching contributions, which can significantly boost your retirement savings.
- **Health Savings Account (HSA):** Contributions to an HSA are tax-deductible, and withdrawals for qualified medical expenses are tax-free. HSAs can also serve as a supplemental retirement account.

Utilizing these accounts can help you save for retirement while reducing your current tax liability. Ensure you understand the contribution limits and eligibility requirements for each account.

Strategies for Reducing Tax Liability

Effective tax planning involves implementing strategies to reduce your overall tax liability. Here are some strategies to consider:

1. **Maximize Deductions:** Take advantage of all available deductions, such as mortgage interest, student loan interest, and charitable contributions. Keeping detailed records and receipts can help you maximize your deductions.
2. **Utilize Tax Credits:** Tax credits directly reduce your tax liability. Common credits include the Earned Income Tax Credit (EITC), Child Tax Credit, and education credits. Research and claim all credits you are eligible for.
3. **Consider Timing of Income and Expenses:** If possible, defer income to a later tax year or accelerate expenses into the current tax year to reduce your taxable income. This strategy can be particularly useful if you expect to be in a lower tax bracket in the future.
4. **Invest in Tax-Efficient Assets:** Consider investing in assets that generate tax-efficient income, such as municipal bonds or index funds. These investments can help reduce your tax liability while growing your wealth.
5. **Charitable Giving:** Donating appreciated assets, such as stocks or real estate, can provide a double tax benefit by avoiding capital gains tax and claiming a charitable deduction for the asset's fair market value.

Implementing these strategies can help you reduce your overall tax liability and keep more of your hard-earned money.

Staying Compliant with Tax Regulations

Staying compliant with tax regulations is essential to avoid penalties and legal issues. Here are some tips for staying compliant:

1. **Keep Accurate Records:** Maintain detailed records of your income, expenses, and tax payments. This includes receipts, invoices, bank statements, and tax forms.
2. **File Taxes on Time:** Ensure you file your tax returns by the required deadlines. For U.S. taxpayers, the tax filing deadline is typically April 15th. If you need more time, file for an extension to avoid late filing penalties.
3. **Understand Foreign Reporting Requirements:** Be aware of additional reporting requirements for foreign accounts and assets, such as the Report of Foreign Bank and Financial Accounts (FBAR) and Form 8938 for the Foreign Account Tax Compliance Act (FATCA).
4. **Stay Informed:** Tax laws and regulations can change frequently. Stay informed about changes that may affect your tax situation and adjust your tax planning strategies accordingly.
5. **Seek Professional Help:** Consider working with a tax professional who specializes in international tax planning. They can provide

personalized advice and ensure you comply with all relevant tax regulations.

By staying compliant with tax regulations, you can avoid potential legal issues and ensure your financial health.

Case Studies and Success Stories

Learning from real-life examples can provide valuable insights into successful tax planning for digital nomads. Here are a couple of case studies:

Case Study 1: Utilizing the FEIE and FTC

Maria, a freelance writer, spent the past year living in Spain while working for clients in the United States. To minimize her U.S. tax liability, Maria took advantage of the Foreign Earned Income Exclusion (FEIE), excluding $112,000 of her foreign-earned income from her taxable income. Additionally, she claimed the Foreign Tax Credit (FTC) for taxes paid to Spain on her remaining income. By utilizing both the FEIE and FTC, Maria significantly reduced her U.S. tax liability while complying with both U.S. and Spanish tax regulations.

Case Study 2: Tax-Efficient Investment Strategy

David, a software developer, maintained a diverse investment portfolio while living as a digital nomad in various countries. To minimize his tax liability, David invested in tax-efficient assets, such as index funds and municipal bonds. He also contributed the maximum amount to his Roth IRA and 401(k) to take advantage of tax-free and tax-deferred growth. By implementing a tax-efficient investment strategy, David was able to grow his wealth while keeping his tax liability low.

Creating a Tax Plan for Digital Nomads

Creating a comprehensive tax plan is essential for managing your tax obligations and optimizing your financial situation. Here are some steps to create a tax plan for digital nomads:

1. **Assess Your Tax Residency:** Determine your tax residency status in each country you reside or earn income. Understand the tax rules and obligations for each jurisdiction.
2. **Identify Applicable Tax Treaties:** Research any tax treaties between your home country and the countries you reside or earn income. Utilize these treaties to avoid double taxation and reduce your tax liability.
3. **Track Your Income and Expenses:** Keep detailed records of your income and expenses, including receipts, invoices, and bank statements. This will help you accurately report your income and claim deductions.

4. **Utilize Tax-Advantaged Accounts:** Contribute to tax-advantaged accounts, such as IRAs, 401(k)s, and HSAs, to reduce your taxable income and grow your savings efficiently.
5. **Plan for Foreign Reporting Requirements:** Ensure you comply with additional reporting requirements for foreign accounts and assets, such as FBAR and FATCA. File the necessary forms and keep accurate records.
6. **Work with a Tax Professional:** Consider working with a tax professional who specializes in international tax planning. They can provide personalized advice and help you create a comprehensive tax plan.

By creating a tax plan, you can effectively manage your tax obligations, reduce your tax liability, and optimize your financial situation as a digital nomad.

Insurance and Risk Management

Insurance and risk management are crucial aspects of personal finance for digital nomads. Ensuring you have adequate coverage and managing potential risks can protect you from financial setbacks and provide peace of mind while living a mobile lifestyle. This chapter will explore essential types of insurance, strategies for managing risks, and tips for choosing the right coverage.

Essential Insurance for Digital Nomads

As a digital nomad, having the right insurance coverage is vital to protect yourself from unforeseen events. Here are some essential types of insurance to consider:

- **Health Insurance:** Health insurance is critical for covering medical expenses, including doctor visits, hospital stays, and prescriptions. As a digital nomad, you can choose between local health insurance plans in your host country or international health insurance that provides coverage worldwide.
- **Travel Insurance:** Travel insurance covers trip cancellations, interruptions, lost or delayed baggage, and emergency medical

expenses. It can provide coverage for short-term trips or extended periods abroad.
- **Life Insurance:** Life insurance provides financial support to your beneficiaries in the event of your death. It can help cover funeral expenses, debts, and provide income replacement for your loved ones.
- **Disability Insurance:** Disability insurance replaces a portion of your income if you become unable to work due to illness or injury. This coverage is essential for protecting your financial stability.
- **Liability Insurance:** Liability insurance protects you from claims of negligence or wrongdoing that result in bodily injury or property damage to others. It can include personal liability, professional liability, and public liability insurance.
- **Home and Renters Insurance:** Home or renters insurance covers your personal belongings against theft, fire, and other perils. It can also provide liability coverage for accidents that occur in your home or rental property.

Having adequate insurance coverage can protect you from financial hardships and ensure you have access to necessary services in case of emergencies.

Health Insurance for Digital Nomads

Health insurance is one of the most critical types of coverage for digital nomads. Here are some options to consider:

- **Local Health Insurance:** Many countries offer health insurance plans for residents, which may include expats and digital nomads. Local health insurance can be more affordable and provide access to local healthcare providers.
- **International Health Insurance:** International health insurance provides coverage worldwide, allowing you to access healthcare services in multiple countries. It often includes emergency medical evacuation and repatriation benefits.
- **Travel Health Insurance:** Travel health insurance provides temporary coverage for medical expenses while traveling. It is suitable for short-term trips but may not offer comprehensive coverage for long-term stays.
- **Telemedicine Services:** Many international health insurance plans offer telemedicine services, allowing you to consult with doctors remotely. This can be a convenient option for non-emergency medical needs.

When choosing health insurance, consider factors such as coverage limits, deductibles, network of providers, and exclusions. Ensure the plan meets your healthcare needs and provides adequate coverage in the countries you plan to visit.

Travel Insurance for Peace of Mind

Travel insurance is essential for protecting yourself against travel-related risks. Here are some key benefits of travel insurance:

- **Trip Cancellation and Interruption:** Travel insurance reimburses you for non-refundable expenses if your trip is canceled or interrupted due to covered reasons, such as illness, natural disasters, or political unrest.
- **Baggage Loss and Delay:** Travel insurance covers the cost of lost, stolen, or delayed baggage. It can provide reimbursement for essential items and help you replace your belongings.
- **Emergency Medical Expenses:** Travel insurance covers medical expenses incurred while traveling, including hospital stays, doctor visits, and emergency medical evacuation.
- **Accidental Death and Dismemberment:** Travel insurance provides a benefit in the event of accidental death or dismemberment during your trip.

When purchasing travel insurance, ensure it covers your specific needs and destinations. Read the policy details carefully to understand the coverage limits, exclusions, and claims process.

Life and Disability Insurance

Life and disability insurance are essential for protecting your financial stability and providing support for your loved ones in case of unexpected events.

- **Life Insurance:** Life insurance provides a death benefit to your beneficiaries, helping them cover expenses such as funeral costs, debts, and income replacement. There are two main types of life insurance: term life insurance, which provides coverage for a specific period, and whole life insurance, which provides lifelong coverage with a cash value component.
- **Disability Insurance:** Disability insurance replaces a portion of your income if you become unable to work due to illness or injury. It can be short-term or long-term, depending on the duration of the coverage. Disability insurance is crucial for protecting your financial stability and ensuring you can meet your living expenses during recovery.

Consider your financial obligations, dependents, and potential loss of income when choosing life and disability insurance coverage. Ensure the policy provides adequate benefits to support your needs and those of your loved ones.

Liability Insurance for Digital Nomads

Liability insurance protects you from financial loss due to claims of negligence or wrongdoing that result in bodily injury or property damage to others. Here are some types of liability insurance to consider:

- **Personal Liability Insurance:** Personal liability insurance covers claims of bodily injury or property damage caused by you or your family members. It can be included in your home or renters insurance policy or purchased separately.
- **Professional Liability Insurance:** Also known as errors and omissions (E&O) insurance, professional liability insurance covers claims of negligence or mistakes in your professional services. This is essential for freelancers and remote workers who provide professional services.
- **Public Liability Insurance:** Public liability insurance covers claims of bodily injury or property damage caused by your business activities. This is important for digital nomads who operate businesses or engage in activities that interact with the public.

Having adequate liability insurance can protect you from financial loss and legal expenses in case of a claim. Ensure the coverage limits are sufficient to cover potential risks and liabilities.

Managing Risks as a Digital Nomad

Effective risk management involves identifying potential risks and implementing strategies to mitigate them. Here are some tips for managing risks as a digital nomad:

1. **Conduct a Risk Assessment:** Identify potential risks related to your lifestyle, such as health emergencies, travel disruptions, and liability issues. Assess the likelihood and impact of each risk.
2. **Create an Emergency Fund:** Build an emergency fund to cover unexpected expenses, such as medical bills, travel disruptions, or lost income. Aim to save at least three to six months' worth of living expenses.
3. **Maintain Health and Safety:** Prioritize your health and safety by adopting a healthy lifestyle, staying informed about local conditions, and following safety guidelines. Regular health check-ups and vaccinations can also help prevent health issues.
4. **Stay Informed:** Keep up-to-date with travel advisories, local regulations, and potential

risks in your destination countries. Stay informed about changes in visa requirements, health risks, and security concerns.
5. **Keep Digital Security in Check:** Protect your digital assets by using strong passwords, enabling two-factor authentication, and keeping your software and devices updated. Consider using a virtual private network (VPN) to secure your internet connection.

By proactively managing risks, you can protect yourself from potential financial setbacks and enjoy a more secure and stress-free digital nomad lifestyle.

Case Studies and Success Stories

Learning from real-life examples can provide valuable insights into effective insurance and risk management for digital nomads. Here are a couple of case studies:

Case Study 1: Comprehensive Health Coverage

Samantha, a freelance graphic designer, prioritized her health while living as a digital nomad. She chose an international health insurance plan that provided coverage worldwide, including emergency medical evacuation. When she experienced a medical emergency in a remote location, her insurance covered the evacuation and medical expenses, ensuring she received the necessary care without financial stress.

Case Study 2: Managing Liability Risks

Michael, a remote software developer, provided professional services to clients worldwide. To protect himself from potential liability claims, he purchased professional liability insurance. When a client filed a claim for a software error, Michael's insurance covered the legal expenses and settlement costs, protecting his financial stability and professional reputation.

Choosing the Right Insurance Coverage

Choosing the right insurance coverage involves evaluating your needs, comparing policies, and understanding the terms and conditions. Here are some tips for selecting the right coverage:

1. **Assess Your Needs:** Identify your specific insurance needs based on your lifestyle, health, profession, and potential risks. Consider factors such as travel frequency, health conditions, and professional liabilities.
2. **Compare Policies:** Research and compare insurance policies from different providers. Look at coverage limits, exclusions, deductibles, and premiums. Ensure the policy meets your needs and provides adequate coverage.
3. **Read the Fine Print:** Carefully read the policy terms and conditions to understand

what is covered and what is excluded. Pay attention to coverage limits, waiting periods, and claim procedures.
4. **Seek Professional Advice:** Consider consulting with an insurance broker or financial advisor who specializes in insurance for digital nomads. They can provide personalized advice and help you choose the right coverage.
5. **Regularly Review Your Coverage:** Periodically review your insurance coverage to ensure it remains adequate and relevant to your changing needs. Update your policies as necessary to reflect changes in your lifestyle or circumstances.

Choosing the right insurance coverage can provide peace of mind and protect you from financial setbacks. Take the time to research and select policies that meet your specific needs.

Financial Planning for Families

Financial planning becomes more complex when you have a family. Ensuring that your loved ones are provided for while maintaining your digital nomad lifestyle requires careful planning and consideration. This chapter will explore budgeting for families, saving for education, managing healthcare and insurance, and estate planning.

Budgeting for Families

Creating a family budget is essential for managing household expenses and achieving financial goals. Here are some steps to create an effective family budget:

1. **Track Income and Expenses:** Start by tracking all sources of income and expenses for at least a month. This includes salaries, freelance income, investments, rent, groceries, utilities, transportation, and childcare.
2. **Set Financial Goals:** Identify short-term and long-term financial goals for your family, such as saving for a home, education, or a vacation. Prioritize these goals and allocate funds accordingly.
3. **Create Spending Categories:** Organize your expenses into categories, such as housing, food, transportation, healthcare, education,

entertainment, and savings. Assign a budget to each category based on your financial goals and priorities.
4. **Review and Adjust:** Regularly review your budget to ensure you are staying on track. Adjust your spending and savings as needed to align with your financial goals and changing circumstances.
5. **Involve the Family:** Involve all family members in the budgeting process. Discuss financial goals, spending habits, and ways to save money. Encouraging open communication can help create a shared sense of responsibility and commitment to the family's financial well-being.

Creating and maintaining a family budget can help you manage expenses, save for future goals, and ensure financial stability for your family.

Saving for Education

Saving for your children's education is an important financial goal for many families. Here are some strategies to help you save for education expenses:

- **529 Plans:** 529 college savings plans offer tax advantages and allow you to save for qualified education expenses. Contributions grow tax-deferred, and withdrawals for qualified expenses are tax-free.
- **Coverdell Education Savings Accounts (ESA):** Coverdell ESAs also offer tax

advantages and can be used for K-12 and higher education expenses. Contributions grow tax-deferred, and withdrawals for qualified expenses are tax-free.
- **Custodial Accounts:** Custodial accounts, such as UTMA/UGMA accounts, allow you to save and invest money for your children. The funds can be used for any purpose but may have tax implications.
- **Regular Savings Accounts:** Setting up a regular savings account dedicated to education expenses can help you systematically save for your children's future education needs.
- **Scholarships and Grants:** Encourage your children to apply for scholarships and grants to help offset education costs. Research available opportunities and assist them in the application process.

Saving for education requires planning and discipline. Start early and regularly contribute to your education savings to ensure you have the funds needed when the time comes.

Managing Healthcare and Insurance

Healthcare and insurance are critical components of financial planning for families. Here are some tips for managing healthcare and insurance needs:

1. **Choose the Right Health Insurance:** Evaluate different health insurance plans to find one that meets your family's needs. Consider coverage options, deductibles, premiums, and network providers.
2. **Regular Health Check-Ups:** Schedule regular health check-ups for all family members to maintain good health and prevent potential health issues. Preventive care can help reduce long-term healthcare costs.
3. **Emergency Fund:** Build an emergency fund to cover unexpected medical expenses. Aim to save at least three to six months' worth of living expenses to provide a financial safety net.
4. **Life and Disability Insurance:** Ensure you have adequate life and disability insurance coverage to protect your family's financial future in case of unexpected events. Review your policies regularly to ensure they meet your family's needs.
5. **Telemedicine Services:** Utilize telemedicine services for non-emergency medical consultations. Telemedicine can provide convenient and cost-effective access to healthcare professionals, especially while traveling.

By managing healthcare and insurance needs effectively, you can ensure your family has access to necessary medical care and is protected from financial hardships due to health-related issues.

Estate Planning

Estate planning is essential for ensuring your family's financial security and protecting your assets. Here are some key components of estate planning:

- **Wills and Trusts:** Create a will to specify how your assets will be distributed upon your death. Consider setting up trusts to manage and protect assets for your beneficiaries.
- **Power of Attorney:** Designate a power of attorney to make financial and legal decisions on your behalf if you become incapacitated. Ensure you choose someone you trust to act in your best interests.
- **Healthcare Directive:** Create a healthcare directive (living will) to outline your medical treatment preferences if you become unable to communicate your wishes. Designate a healthcare proxy to make medical decisions on your behalf.
- **Beneficiary Designations:** Review and update beneficiary designations on your insurance policies, retirement accounts, and other financial assets. Ensure they align with your estate planning goals.
- **Guardianship Designations:** If you have minor children, designate a guardian to care for them in case of your death. Ensure the designated guardian is willing and able to take on this responsibility.

Estate planning provides peace of mind and ensures your family is cared for and your assets are distributed according to your wishes. Consult with an estate planning attorney to create a comprehensive plan that meets your needs.

Balancing Work and Family Life

Balancing work and family life can be challenging for digital nomads. Here are some tips to help you achieve a healthy balance:

1. **Set Boundaries:** Establish clear boundaries between work and family time. Create a dedicated workspace and set specific work hours to minimize distractions and maintain productivity.
2. **Prioritize Family Time:** Make time for family activities and prioritize spending quality time with your loved ones. Schedule regular family outings, vacations, and activities to strengthen family bonds.
3. **Involve Your Family:** Involve your family in your travel plans and work schedule. Discuss destinations, activities, and work commitments to ensure everyone's needs and preferences are considered.
4. **Delegate Tasks:** Delegate household tasks and responsibilities to family members to share the workload. Encourage teamwork and collaboration to create a supportive and cooperative family environment.

5. **Stay Connected:** Use technology to stay connected with extended family and friends. Regular video calls, messages, and social media can help maintain relationships and provide a support network.

Achieving a healthy work-life balance requires communication, planning, and flexibility. By prioritizing family time and setting boundaries, you can create a fulfilling and harmonious family life.

Case Studies and Success Stories

Learning from real-life examples can provide valuable insights into effective financial planning for families. Here are a couple of case studies:

Case Study 1: Budgeting for a Growing Family

Sarah and Tom, both remote workers, decided to start a family while continuing their digital nomad lifestyle. They created a detailed family budget, accounting for expenses such as healthcare, childcare, and education savings. By prioritizing their financial goals and involving their children in budgeting discussions, Sarah and Tom were able to achieve financial stability and provide a nurturing environment for their growing family.

Case Study 2: Saving for Education

Jessica, a freelance writer, wanted to ensure her children had access to quality education. She set up 529 college savings plans for each of her children and made regular contributions. Jessica also encouraged her children to apply for scholarships and grants to help cover education costs. Through careful planning and disciplined saving, Jessica was able to fund her children's education without compromising her financial stability.

Navigating Banking and Currency Issues

As a digital nomad, managing your finances across multiple countries involves dealing with various banking and currency challenges. This chapter will explore strategies for efficient banking, managing currency exchange, and utilizing financial tools to streamline your financial operations.

Choosing the Right Bank

Choosing the right bank is essential for managing your finances while living a mobile lifestyle. Here are some factors to consider when selecting a bank:

- **International Accessibility:** Choose a bank with a strong international presence and accessibility. Look for banks that offer online banking, international ATM access, and global customer service.
- **Low Fees:** Compare fees for services such as international transfers, ATM withdrawals, and account maintenance. Opt for banks that offer low or no fees for these services.
- **Multi-Currency Accounts:** Consider banks that offer multi-currency accounts, allowing you to hold and manage funds in different currencies. This can simplify currency exchange and reduce conversion fees.

- **Security:** Ensure the bank has robust security measures in place to protect your funds and personal information. Look for features such as two-factor authentication, fraud detection, and secure online banking platforms.

Research and compare different banks to find one that meets your needs and offers the best combination of features and services for your lifestyle.

Managing Currency Exchange

Currency exchange can significantly impact your finances, especially if you frequently move between countries. Here are some tips for managing currency exchange efficiently:

1. **Use Multi-Currency Accounts:** Multi-currency accounts allow you to hold funds in multiple currencies, reducing the need for frequent conversions. This can help you take advantage of favorable exchange rates and minimize conversion fees.
2. **Monitor Exchange Rates:** Keep an eye on exchange rates and make conversions when rates are favorable. Use currency exchange apps and websites to stay updated on current rates.
3. **Utilize Transfer Services:** Use international money transfer services like Wise (formerly TransferWise), Revolut, and PayPal to transfer funds between accounts. These

services often offer better exchange rates and lower fees compared to traditional banks.
4. **Avoid Airport Exchanges:** Avoid exchanging currency at airports, as they often offer poor exchange rates and high fees. Use ATMs or local banks for better rates.
5. **Plan Ahead:** Plan your currency needs in advance and exchange larger amounts at once to reduce the impact of fees. This can help you manage your finances more efficiently.

By managing currency exchange effectively, you can minimize costs and maximize the value of your funds while traveling.

Utilizing Financial Tools and Apps

There are numerous financial tools and apps available to help digital nomads manage their finances. Here are some recommended tools:

- **Budgeting Apps:** Mint, YNAB (You Need A Budget), and PocketGuard can help you track expenses, create budgets, and manage your finances efficiently.
- **Expense Tracking Apps:** Expensify, Trail Wallet, and Money Lover are great for tracking and categorizing expenses, making it easier to monitor your spending habits.
- **Banking Apps:** Mobile banking apps from your bank provide easy access to your

accounts, allowing you to transfer funds, pay bills, and monitor transactions on the go.
- **Currency Exchange Apps:** XE Currency, Currency Converter Plus, and Revolut can help you monitor exchange rates and make currency conversions easily.
- **Investment Apps:** Robinhood, Betterment, and Acorns allow you to manage and grow your investments from anywhere in the world.
- **Transfer Services:** Wise, PayPal, and Western Union enable quick and cost-effective international money transfers.

Utilizing these tools can streamline your financial management and help you stay on top of your finances while living a nomadic lifestyle.

Setting Up a Home Base

Having a financial home base can simplify your banking and currency management. Here are some benefits of setting up a home base:

- **Consistent Banking:** Maintaining a primary bank account in your home country or a country with a stable banking system provides consistency and reliability.
- **Stable Currency:** Holding funds in a stable currency can protect you from exchange rate fluctuations and economic instability in other countries.
- **Legal and Tax Considerations:** A home base can simplify legal and tax obligations,

providing a clear point of reference for tax residency and reporting.
- **Address for Correspondence:** A home base provides a permanent address for banking correspondence, legal documents, and other important communications.

Choose a home base that offers financial stability, favorable tax conditions, and reliable banking services to support your nomadic lifestyle.

Dealing with Financial Emergencies

Financial emergencies can occur unexpectedly, and being prepared is crucial. Here are some tips for dealing with financial emergencies:

1. **Build an Emergency Fund:** Save at least three to six months' worth of living expenses in an easily accessible account. This fund can cover unexpected expenses such as medical bills, travel disruptions, or lost income.
2. **Maintain Multiple Accounts:** Keep accounts in different banks and countries to ensure you have access to funds in case of banking issues or restrictions.
3. **Have Backup Payment Methods:** Carry multiple payment methods, such as credit cards, debit cards, and cash, to ensure you can make payments in various situations.

4. **Stay Informed:** Stay updated on potential risks and disruptions in your destination countries. Monitor local news, travel advisories, and financial updates to stay prepared.
5. **Insurance Coverage:** Ensure you have adequate insurance coverage, including travel insurance, health insurance, and liability insurance, to protect yourself from financial losses.

By being prepared for financial emergencies, you can mitigate the impact of unexpected events and maintain financial stability.

Case Studies and Success Stories

Learning from real-life examples can provide valuable insights into effective banking and currency management for digital nomads. Here are a couple of case studies:

Case Study 1: Efficient Currency Management

Alex, a freelance photographer, frequently traveled between Europe and Asia. To manage currency exchange efficiently, Alex opened a multi-currency account with a bank that offered favorable exchange rates and low fees. He used a currency exchange app to monitor rates and made conversions when rates were favorable. By managing his currency exchange strategically, Alex saved money on conversion fees and maximized the value of his funds.

Case Study 2: Utilizing Financial Tools

Laura, a remote software developer, used various financial tools to streamline her financial management. She tracked her expenses with a budgeting app, used an international money transfer service for client payments, and monitored exchange rates with a currency exchange app. By leveraging these tools, Laura was able to manage her finances efficiently and focus on her work and travels.

Building and Maintaining Credit on the Road

Maintaining a strong credit profile is crucial for financial health, even for digital nomads. Good credit can help you secure loans, rent apartments, and obtain favorable interest rates. This chapter will explore strategies for building and maintaining good credit while living a mobile lifestyle.

Understanding Credit Scores and Reports

Credit scores are numerical representations of your creditworthiness, based on your credit history. They range from 300 to 850, with higher scores indicating better credit. Key factors that influence your credit score include:

- **Payment History:** Your track record of making on-time payments.
- **Credit Utilization:** The ratio of your credit card balances to your credit limits.
- **Length of Credit History:** The age of your credit accounts.
- **New Credit Inquiries:** The number of recent applications for new credit.

- **Credit Mix:** The variety of credit accounts you have, such as credit cards, loans, and mortgages.

Your credit report is a detailed record of your credit history, including credit accounts, payment history, and inquiries. Regularly reviewing your credit report can help you spot errors and detect signs of identity theft early.

Strategies for Building Good Credit

Building good credit requires consistent and responsible financial behavior. Here are some strategies to help you build and maintain a strong credit profile:

1. **Pay Your Bills on Time:** Your payment history is the most significant factor in your credit score. Always pay your bills on time to avoid late payments and penalties.
2. **Keep Credit Utilization Low:** Aim to keep your credit utilization below 30%. High credit utilization can negatively impact your credit score.
3. **Maintain Long-Term Credit Accounts:** The length of your credit history matters. Keep older accounts open, even if you don't use them frequently, to establish a longer credit history.

4. **Avoid Opening Too Many New Accounts:** Each time you apply for new credit, it results in a hard inquiry, which can temporarily lower your credit score. Avoid opening multiple new accounts in a short period.
5. **Monitor Your Credit Report:** Regularly check your credit report for errors or fraudulent activity. Dispute any inaccuracies with the credit bureaus to keep your credit report accurate.
6. **Use a Secured Credit Card:** If you're new to credit or rebuilding credit, consider using a secured credit card. Secured cards require a deposit, which serves as your credit limit and reduces the risk for the issuer.

By following these strategies, you can build and maintain a strong credit profile, which is essential for achieving your financial goals.

Managing Credit While Traveling

Managing credit while traveling can be challenging, but it is possible with careful planning and organization. Here are some tips for managing your credit on the road:

1. **Set Up Automatic Payments:** Set up automatic payments for your credit cards and other bills to ensure they are paid on time, even when you're traveling.

2. **Monitor Your Accounts:** Regularly check your credit card accounts and credit report for suspicious activity. Use mobile banking apps and online account management tools to stay on top of your finances.
3. **Notify Your Credit Card Issuers:** Inform your credit card issuers of your travel plans to avoid having your card flagged for suspicious activity. This can prevent your card from being declined while you're abroad.
4. **Use a VPN:** Use a virtual private network (VPN) to secure your internet connection when accessing your financial accounts online. This can protect your personal information from hackers.
5. **Keep Backup Payment Methods:** Carry multiple payment methods, such as credit cards, debit cards, and cash, to ensure you have access to funds in case of an emergency.

By staying organized and proactive, you can effectively manage your credit while enjoying your digital nomad lifestyle.

Dealing with Credit Challenges

Even with careful planning, you may encounter credit challenges while traveling. Here are some tips for dealing with common credit issues:

- **Addressing Late Payments:** If you miss a payment, contact your creditor as soon as possible to explain the situation. They may be

willing to waive late fees or work out a payment plan.
- **Handling Credit Card Fraud:** If you suspect fraudulent activity on your credit card, contact your issuer immediately to report the fraud and have the card replaced. Regularly monitoring your accounts can help you catch fraud early.
- **Rebuilding Credit:** If your credit score has been damaged, focus on rebuilding it by making on-time payments, reducing credit card balances, and avoiding new credit inquiries. Consider using a secured credit card or a credit-builder loan to help improve your credit.

Dealing with credit challenges requires patience and persistence. By taking proactive steps, you can overcome these challenges and maintain a healthy credit profile.

Leveraging Credit for Financial Growth

Good credit can open doors to various financial opportunities, including loans, mortgages, and better interest rates. Here are some ways to leverage your good credit for financial growth:

1. **Secure Better Loan Terms:** With good credit, you can qualify for loans with lower interest rates and better terms. This can save

you money on interest payments and help you achieve your financial goals faster.
2. **Access Higher Credit Limits:** A strong credit profile can lead to higher credit limits, giving you more financial flexibility. Be sure to use this increased credit responsibly to maintain your credit score.
3. **Invest in Real Estate:** Good credit can help you qualify for mortgages and real estate loans, allowing you to invest in property and build wealth through real estate.
4. **Start a Business:** If you plan to start your own business, good credit can help you secure business loans and lines of credit. This can provide the necessary capital to launch and grow your business.

Leveraging your good credit can help you achieve your financial goals and build a secure financial future.

Case Studies and Success Stories

Learning from real-life examples can provide valuable insights into building and maintaining good credit as a digital nomad. Here are a couple of case studies:

Case Study 1: Building Credit with a Secured Credit Card

Emma, a recent college graduate and new digital nomad, had limited credit history. She opened a secured credit card with a $500 deposit and used it responsibly for everyday purchases. By paying her balance in full each month and keeping her credit utilization low, Emma built a positive credit history. After a year, her credit score improved, and she was able to qualify for an unsecured credit card with a higher limit.

Case Study 2: Managing Credit While Traveling

James, a freelance writer, traveled extensively for work. To manage his credit, he set up automatic payments for all his bills and monitored his accounts regularly using mobile banking apps. When he noticed a fraudulent charge on his credit card, he immediately contacted his issuer to report the fraud and had the card replaced. By staying proactive and organized, James maintained a strong credit profile and enjoyed financial flexibility while traveling.

Investing for Digital Nomads

Investing is a powerful tool for growing your wealth and achieving financial independence. For digital nomads, investing requires a strategic approach that accommodates a mobile lifestyle. This chapter will explore investment principles, different types of investments, and strategies for building and managing an investment portfolio while living a nomadic lifestyle.

Introduction to Investing

Investing involves allocating money to assets or ventures with the expectation of generating a profit or income. Unlike saving, which focuses on preserving capital, investing aims to grow your wealth by taking on calculated risks. Understanding the fundamentals of investing is crucial for making informed decisions and achieving long-term financial goals.

The primary goal of investing is to build wealth over time through compound interest, capital appreciation, and income generation. Whether you're investing in stocks, bonds, real estate, or other assets, the key is to start early, invest consistently, and stay informed about market trends and opportunities.

Types of Investments

There are various types of investments, each with its own risk and return characteristics. As a digital nomad, it's important to choose investments that align with your financial goals, risk tolerance, and lifestyle. Here are some common types of investments:

- **Stocks:** Stocks represent ownership in a company. Investing in stocks can provide capital appreciation and dividend income. While stocks can offer high returns, they also come with higher risk and volatility.
- **Bonds:** Bonds are debt securities issued by governments, municipalities, or corporations. They provide regular interest payments and return the principal at maturity. Bonds are generally considered lower-risk investments compared to stocks.
- **Mutual Funds:** Mutual funds pool money from multiple investors to invest in a diversified portfolio of stocks, bonds, or other securities. They offer diversification and professional management but come with management fees.
- **Exchange-Traded Funds (ETFs):** ETFs are similar to mutual funds but trade on stock exchanges like individual stocks. They offer diversification, liquidity, and typically lower fees than mutual funds.
- **Real Estate:** Real estate investments include residential, commercial, and rental properties. Real estate can provide rental income, capital

appreciation, and diversification. However, it requires significant capital and management.
- **Cryptocurrencies:** Cryptocurrencies are digital or virtual currencies that use cryptography for security. Investing in cryptocurrencies can offer high returns but comes with high volatility and regulatory risks.

Diversifying your investments across different asset classes can help spread risk and increase the potential for returns. The right mix of investments depends on your financial goals, risk tolerance, and investment horizon.

Risk Management and Diversification

Risk management is a crucial aspect of investing. While all investments carry some level of risk, understanding and managing these risks can help protect your portfolio and achieve your financial goals. Here are some key risk management strategies:

1. **Diversification:** Diversification involves spreading your investments across different asset classes, sectors, and geographic regions to reduce risk. A diversified portfolio can help mitigate the impact of poor performance in any single investment.
2. **Asset Allocation:** Asset allocation is the process of determining the optimal mix of

asset classes in your portfolio based on your risk tolerance, financial goals, and investment horizon. Regularly review and rebalance your asset allocation to stay aligned with your objectives.
3. **Risk Assessment:** Understand the risk profile of each investment and how it fits into your overall portfolio. Assess factors such as market risk, interest rate risk, inflation risk, and credit risk.
4. **Stop-Loss Orders:** Stop-loss orders are instructions to sell a security when its price reaches a certain level. They can help limit potential losses and protect your investment capital.
5. **Hedging:** Hedging involves using financial instruments, such as options or futures, to offset potential losses in your investments. While hedging can reduce risk, it also comes with costs and complexities.

By implementing these risk management strategies, you can build a resilient investment portfolio that withstands market fluctuations and achieves your long-term financial goals.

Building an Investment Portfolio

Building an investment portfolio involves selecting and managing a collection of investments that align with your financial goals and risk tolerance. Here are the key steps to building a successful investment portfolio:

1. **Define Your Investment Goals:** Identify your short-term and long-term financial goals. Determine the purpose of your investments, whether it's for retirement, buying a home, or achieving financial independence.
2. **Assess Your Risk Tolerance:** Understand your risk tolerance, which is your ability and willingness to take on risk. Consider factors such as your financial situation, investment horizon, and emotional comfort with market volatility.
3. **Determine Your Asset Allocation:** Based on your risk tolerance and investment goals, decide on the optimal mix of asset classes in your portfolio. A common approach is to allocate a percentage of your portfolio to stocks, bonds, and other assets.
4. **Select Your Investments:** Choose individual investments or investment funds that align with your asset allocation strategy. Research and evaluate each investment based on factors such as performance, fees, and risk profile.
5. **Monitor and Rebalance Your Portfolio:** Regularly review your portfolio to ensure it remains aligned with your investment goals and risk tolerance. Rebalance your portfolio by buying or selling investments to maintain your desired asset allocation.
6. **Stay Informed:** Stay informed about market trends, economic developments, and changes in your investments. Continuously educate yourself about investing to make informed

decisions and adapt to changing market conditions.

Building and managing an investment portfolio requires discipline, patience, and a long-term perspective. By following these steps, you can create a diversified portfolio that supports your financial goals and provides growth opportunities.

Investing for Passive Income

As a digital nomad, generating passive income can provide financial stability and freedom. Passive income is earnings derived from investments that require minimal effort to maintain. Here are some popular passive income investments:

- **Dividend Stocks:** Dividend stocks are shares of companies that pay regular dividends to shareholders. Investing in dividend stocks can provide a steady stream of income and potential capital appreciation.
- **Real Estate Investment Trusts (REITs):** REITs are companies that own and operate income-generating real estate. They pay regular dividends to investors and offer a way to invest in real estate without owning physical properties.
- **Peer-to-Peer Lending:** Peer-to-peer lending platforms connect borrowers with individual lenders. Investors earn interest on the loans they fund, generating passive income.

- **Bond Investments:** Bonds provide regular interest payments to investors. While they may offer lower returns than stocks, they are generally less volatile and provide stable income.
- **Index Funds and ETFs:** Index funds and ETFs that focus on dividend-paying stocks or high-yield bonds can provide passive income while offering diversification and professional management.

Investing for passive income can help you achieve financial independence and support your nomadic lifestyle. By diversifying your passive income sources, you can create a reliable income stream that allows you to focus on your passions and adventures.

Tax Considerations for Digital Nomads

As a digital nomad, understanding the tax implications of your investments is crucial for maximizing your returns and staying compliant with tax regulations. Here are some key tax considerations:

- **Tax-Advantaged Accounts:** Take advantage of tax-advantaged accounts such as IRAs, Roth IRAs, and 401(k)s. These accounts offer tax benefits that can help grow your investments more efficiently.
- **Capital Gains Tax:** Understand the capital gains tax rates for your investments. Long-

term capital gains (investments held for more than a year) are typically taxed at lower rates than short-term capital gains.
- **Foreign Tax Credits:** If you earn investment income in foreign countries, you may be eligible for foreign tax credits. These credits can help offset taxes paid to other countries, reducing your overall tax liability.
- **Double Taxation Agreements:** Research double taxation agreements between your home country and the countries you reside in. These agreements can prevent double taxation on your investment income.
- **Reporting Requirements:** Stay informed about the reporting requirements for your investments, including foreign assets and accounts. Failure to comply with reporting obligations can result in penalties and fines.

Consulting with a tax professional who specializes in international tax can help you navigate the complexities of tax planning and ensure you optimize your tax strategy for your investments.

Case Studies and Success Stories

Learning from real-life examples can provide valuable insights into successful investing for digital nomads. Here are a couple of case studies:

Case Study 1: From Rental Property to Real Estate Empire

Emily, a digital nomad and freelance writer, started her real estate journey by purchasing a small rental property in her hometown. With a keen eye for undervalued properties and a knack for property management, Emily quickly turned her first investment into a profitable venture. She reinvested the rental income into additional properties, leveraging financing options to expand her portfolio. Today, Emily owns a diverse range of rental properties across multiple states, generating significant passive income that supports her nomadic lifestyle.

Case Study 2: Investing in Dividend Stocks

David, a remote software developer, focused on building a portfolio of dividend-paying stocks. By researching companies with strong financials and consistent dividend payouts, David created a diversified portfolio that generated a steady stream of passive income. He reinvested the dividends to purchase more shares, compounding his returns over time. This strategy allowed David to achieve financial independence and enjoy his digital nomad lifestyle without worrying about regular income.

Planning for Long-Term Financial Goals

Effective investing requires planning for long-term financial goals, such as retirement, buying a home, or funding education. Here are some tips for planning for your long-term financial goals:

1. **Set Clear Goals:** Define your long-term financial goals and set specific, measurable, achievable, relevant, and time-bound (SMART) objectives.
2. **Create a Financial Plan:** Develop a comprehensive financial plan that includes budgeting, saving, investing, and risk management strategies. Use financial tools and apps to help you stay organized and on track.
3. **Review and Adjust Regularly:** Monitor your progress towards your financial goals regularly. Adjust your plan as needed to stay aligned with your objectives and adapt to changes in your financial situation.
4. **Seek Professional Advice:** Consider working with a financial advisor to help you create and implement a robust financial plan. They can provide personalized advice and support based on your unique circumstances and goals.

By planning for your long-term financial goals and investing wisely, you can achieve financial security and enjoy a fulfilling digital nomad lifestyle.

Achieving Financial Independence

Financial independence is the ultimate goal for many people, including digital nomads. It represents the ability to live comfortably without being dependent on employment income. This chapter will explore the concept of financial independence, strategies to accelerate your journey toward financial freedom, case studies of financially independent individuals, and tips for maintaining wealth and financial health.

The Concept of Financial Independence

Financial independence means having sufficient personal wealth to cover your living expenses without relying on active income from work. It provides the freedom to pursue passions, hobbies, and interests without the financial pressure of a job. Key components of financial independence include:

- **Passive Income:** Income generated from investments, rental properties, or other sources that require minimal effort to maintain.
- **Financial Security:** Having enough savings and investments to cover emergencies and unexpected expenses.

- **Debt Freedom:** Being free from high-interest debt, which can drain financial resources and limit your ability to save and invest.
- **Living Below Your Means:** Spending less than you earn and saving or investing the difference.

Achieving financial independence requires disciplined saving, smart investing, and strategic planning. It is a long-term goal that can provide significant lifestyle benefits and peace of mind.

Strategies for Accelerating Financial Freedom

While achieving financial independence takes time, there are strategies you can implement to accelerate the process. Here are some effective strategies:

1. **Increase Your Savings Rate:** Aim to save a substantial portion of your income. The higher your savings rate, the faster you can build your investment portfolio and reach financial independence.
2. **Invest Wisely:** Invest in a diversified portfolio of stocks, bonds, real estate, and other assets that align with your risk tolerance and financial goals. Focus on investments that provide passive income and capital appreciation.
3. **Minimize Expenses:** Cut unnecessary expenses and live frugally. Focus on spending

money on things that truly matter to you and provide value.
4. **Generate Multiple Income Streams:** Diversify your income sources by creating multiple streams of passive income, such as rental properties, dividend-paying stocks, or a side business.
5. **Pay Off Debt:** Prioritize paying off high-interest debt to free up more money for saving and investing. Avoid accumulating new debt whenever possible.
6. **Leverage Tax-Advantaged Accounts:** Take advantage of retirement accounts like 401(k)s, IRAs, and HSAs, which offer tax benefits and help your investments grow more efficiently.
7. **Stay Educated:** Continuously educate yourself about personal finance, investing, and money management. Knowledge is a powerful tool for making informed financial decisions.

By implementing these strategies, you can accelerate your journey toward financial independence and enjoy the freedom and flexibility it offers.

Case Studies of Financially Independent Individuals

Learning from real-life examples can provide valuable insights and inspiration for your own financial independence journey. Here are two case studies of individuals who achieved financial independence:

Case Study 1: Early Retirement through Real Estate Investing

Mark, a software engineer, started investing in real estate in his late twenties. He purchased rental properties in high-demand areas, carefully managing and maintaining them to ensure steady rental income. By the time Mark was 40, he had built a substantial portfolio of rental properties generating enough passive income to cover his living expenses. This allowed him to retire early and focus on his passions, including travel and philanthropy.

Case Study 2: Financial Independence through Frugality and Investing

Jane, a graphic designer, was determined to achieve financial independence by the age of 45. She adopted a frugal lifestyle, meticulously tracking her expenses and cutting unnecessary costs. Jane invested aggressively in index funds and dividend-paying stocks, reinvesting the dividends to accelerate growth. By maintaining a high savings rate and making smart investment choices, Jane reached her financial independence goal and now enjoys a flexible lifestyle, pursuing her creative interests without financial constraints.

Maintaining Wealth and Financial Health

Achieving financial independence is a significant milestone, but maintaining wealth and financial health is equally important. Here are some tips to ensure long-term financial stability:

1. **Continue Investing:** Keep your investments diversified and regularly review your portfolio to ensure it remains aligned with your financial goals and risk tolerance.
2. **Live Below Your Means:** Continue to live frugally and avoid lifestyle inflation. Prioritize spending on experiences and items that bring lasting value and happiness.
3. **Maintain an Emergency Fund:** Keep a robust emergency fund to cover unexpected expenses and provide a financial safety net.
4. **Plan for Healthcare Costs:** Anticipate and plan for healthcare expenses in retirement. Consider health insurance options and potential long-term care needs.
5. **Stay Informed:** Keep up-to-date with financial news, market trends, and changes in tax laws. Staying informed helps you make proactive and informed financial decisions.
6. **Review Your Financial Plan:** Regularly review and update your financial plan to ensure it reflects your current goals and circumstances. Adjust your strategies as needed to stay on track.

7. **Consult Financial Professionals:** Work with financial advisors, tax professionals, and estate planners to optimize your financial strategies and ensure you are making the best decisions for your situation.

Maintaining wealth and financial health requires ongoing effort and vigilance. By following these tips, you can enjoy the benefits of financial independence while ensuring long-term financial stability.

Dealing with Financial Challenges

Financial challenges are a part of life, and knowing how to navigate them effectively is crucial for maintaining financial stability. This chapter will explore strategies for dealing with financial crises, handling unexpected expenses, rebuilding after financial setbacks, and accessing resources for financial assistance.

Navigating Financial Crises

Financial crises can arise from various situations, such as job loss, medical emergencies, economic downturns, or unexpected major expenses. Here are some steps to navigate financial crises effectively:

1. **Assess the Situation:** Take a step back and evaluate the full extent of the financial crisis. Identify the root cause, the immediate impact on your finances, and potential long-term effects.
2. **Create a Crisis Budget:** Develop a temporary budget that focuses on essential expenses only. Cut non-essential spending and prioritize necessities like housing, utilities, food, and healthcare.
3. **Seek Support:** Reach out to family, friends, or support groups for emotional and practical

assistance. Sometimes talking to others can provide new perspectives and solutions.
4. **Communicate with Creditors:** Contact your creditors to explain your situation and negotiate temporary payment arrangements or deferments. Many creditors are willing to work with you during difficult times.
5. **Utilize Emergency Savings:** If you have an emergency fund, use it to cover essential expenses. This is what the fund is for, and it can provide a financial cushion while you navigate the crisis.
6. **Explore Financial Assistance Programs:** Research available financial assistance programs, such as unemployment benefits, government aid, or non-profit organizations that offer support during crises.

By taking proactive steps and seeking support, you can navigate financial crises with greater resilience and minimize the long-term impact on your finances.

Strategies for Handling Unexpected Expenses

Unexpected expenses, such as car repairs, medical bills, or home maintenance, can disrupt your financial plans. Here are strategies to handle unexpected expenses effectively:

1. **Build an Emergency Fund:** Aim to save at least three to six months' worth of living expenses in an easily accessible account. This

fund can cover unexpected costs and provide a financial safety net.
2. **Use a Budget Buffer:** Include a buffer in your monthly budget for unexpected expenses. This can help absorb smaller unexpected costs without disrupting your overall financial plan.
3. **Prioritize Expenses:** When faced with unexpected costs, prioritize your expenses and determine which ones can be postponed or reduced. Focus on essential expenses first.
4. **Negotiate Payment Plans:** If the unexpected expense is significant, negotiate a payment plan with the service provider. This can make the cost more manageable and spread out the payments over time.
5. **Utilize Credit Wisely:** If you need to use credit to cover an unexpected expense, choose the option with the lowest interest rate and create a repayment plan to pay off the debt as quickly as possible.
6. **Review Insurance Coverage:** Regularly review your insurance policies to ensure you have adequate coverage for potential unexpected expenses, such as health, auto, and home insurance.

By implementing these strategies, you can handle unexpected expenses with less stress and maintain your financial stability.

Rebuilding After Financial Setbacks

Financial setbacks, such as job loss, bankruptcy, or significant debt, can be challenging to overcome. However, with a strategic approach, you can rebuild your financial health. Here are steps to help you recover from financial setbacks:

1. **Assess the Damage:** Evaluate the full extent of the financial setback, including debts, missed payments, and the impact on your credit score. Understanding the scope of the issue is the first step to recovery.
2. **Create a Recovery Plan:** Develop a detailed plan to address the financial setback. This may include budgeting, debt repayment strategies, and steps to rebuild your credit.
3. **Reduce Expenses:** Cut non-essential expenses and focus on reducing your overall spending. Redirect the saved funds towards debt repayment and rebuilding your savings.
4. **Increase Income:** Look for opportunities to increase your income, such as taking on a part-time job, freelancing, or selling unused items. Additional income can accelerate your financial recovery.
5. **Focus on Debt Repayment:** Prioritize paying off high-interest debt first to reduce the overall cost of your debt. Consider debt consolidation or seeking professional advice if needed.

6. **Rebuild Your Credit:** Take steps to improve your credit score, such as making on-time payments, reducing credit card balances, and avoiding new debt. Regularly monitor your credit report for errors or inaccuracies.
7. **Seek Professional Help:** Consider working with a financial advisor or credit counselor to create a tailored recovery plan and provide guidance throughout the process.

Rebuilding after financial setbacks takes time and effort, but with determination and a clear plan, you can restore your financial health and achieve long-term stability.

Resources for Financial Assistance

Various resources are available to help you navigate financial challenges and access financial assistance. Here are some valuable resources to consider:

- **Government Assistance Programs:** Many governments offer programs to assist individuals facing financial hardship. Examples include unemployment benefits, food assistance programs, and housing support.
- **Non-Profit Organizations:** Non-profit organizations often provide financial assistance, counseling, and support services.

Examples include the Salvation Army, United Way, and local community organizations.
- **Credit Counseling Services:** Credit counseling agencies can help you develop a debt repayment plan, negotiate with creditors, and provide financial education. Look for accredited agencies through organizations like the National Foundation for Credit Counseling (NFCC).
- **Financial Advisors:** Professional financial advisors can offer personalized advice and create tailored financial plans to help you navigate challenges and achieve your goals.
- **Online Financial Tools and Resources:** Numerous online tools and resources can assist with budgeting, debt management, and financial planning. Websites like Mint, NerdWallet, and Credit Karma offer valuable information and tools.
- **Community Resources:** Local community centers, religious organizations, and social service agencies often offer financial assistance programs and support services. Check with local resources for available options.

Utilizing these resources can provide valuable support and guidance during financial challenges, helping you achieve stability and regain control of your finances.

Behavioral Finance and Money Psychology

Behavioral finance explores the psychological influences and biases that affect financial decision-making. Understanding these factors can help you make better financial choices and achieve long-term financial success. This chapter will delve into understanding your financial behavior, overcoming psychological barriers to financial success, building healthy money habits, and practicing mindfulness for financial well-being.

Understanding Your Financial Behavior

Understanding your financial behavior involves recognizing the psychological factors that influence your financial decisions. Here are some common psychological biases and behaviors that can impact your financial choices:

- **Anchoring:** The tendency to rely heavily on the first piece of information encountered (the "anchor") when making decisions. For example, the initial price of an item can influence your perception of its value.
- **Loss Aversion:** The tendency to prefer avoiding losses over acquiring equivalent

gains. This can lead to risk-averse behavior and impact investment decisions.
- **Overconfidence:** Overestimating your knowledge or ability to predict financial outcomes. This can lead to excessive risk-taking and poor investment choices.
- **Herd Behavior:** The tendency to follow the actions of a larger group, even if those actions may not be rational. This can lead to market bubbles and investment in overvalued assets.**Confirmation Bias:** The tendency to seek out information that confirms your existing beliefs and ignore information that contradicts them. This can result in biased decision-making and poor financial choices.
- **Short-Term Focus:** The tendency to prioritize immediate gratification over long-term goals. This can lead to overspending and inadequate saving for future needs.

By recognizing these biases and understanding how they influence your financial behavior, you can make more informed and rational financial decisions.

Overcoming Psychological Barriers to Financial Success

Overcoming psychological barriers is crucial for achieving financial success. Here are some strategies to help you address common psychological obstacles:

1. **Set Clear Financial Goals:** Define specific, measurable, achievable, relevant, and time-bound (SMART) financial goals. Clear goals provide direction and motivation for your financial decisions.
2. **Develop a Financial Plan:** Create a comprehensive financial plan that outlines your income, expenses, savings, investments, and debt management strategies. A well-structured plan can help you stay focused and disciplined.
3. **Practice Self-Awareness:** Reflect on your financial behavior and identify any biases or habits that may hinder your progress. Self-awareness allows you to recognize and address these issues proactively.
4. **Seek Professional Advice:** Consult with financial advisors, counselors, or coaches to gain an objective perspective and receive personalized guidance. Professional advice can help you navigate complex financial decisions.
5. **Embrace Long-Term Thinking:** Shift your focus from short-term gratification to long-term goals. Visualize the benefits of achieving your financial goals and remind yourself of the importance of delayed gratification.
6. **Stay Educated:** Continuously educate yourself about personal finance, investing, and money management. Knowledge empowers you to make informed decisions and overcome psychological barriers.

By implementing these strategies, you can overcome psychological barriers and set yourself on the path to financial success.

Building Healthy Money Habits

Building healthy money habits is essential for long-term financial well-being. Here are some tips to help you develop and maintain positive financial habits:

1. **Create a Budget:** Develop a budget that outlines your income, expenses, and savings goals. Regularly track your spending to ensure you stay within your budget and make adjustments as needed.
2. **Automate Savings:** Set up automatic transfers to your savings and investment accounts. Automating your savings ensures consistency and helps you prioritize saving over spending.
3. **Pay Yourself First:** Prioritize saving and investing a portion of your income before allocating money to other expenses. This helps you build wealth and achieve your financial goals.
4. **Reduce Debt:** Focus on paying off high-interest debt as quickly as possible. Avoid accumulating new debt and use credit responsibly to maintain a healthy financial position.
5. **Invest Regularly:** Make regular contributions to your investment accounts, regardless of market conditions. Consistent investing helps

you take advantage of compound interest and grow your wealth over time.
6. **Review and Adjust:** Regularly review your financial plan, budget, and goals. Make adjustments as needed to stay on track and adapt to changes in your financial situation.

By building and maintaining healthy money habits, you can create a strong financial foundation and achieve long-term financial stability.

Mindfulness and Financial Well-being

Practicing mindfulness can enhance your financial well-being by promoting self-awareness and intentional decision-making. Here are some mindfulness practices to improve your financial health:

1. **Mindful Spending:** Before making a purchase, pause and consider whether it aligns with your values and financial goals. Avoid impulsive spending and focus on intentional, value-driven purchases.
2. **Gratitude:** Cultivate gratitude for what you have rather than focusing on what you lack. Practicing gratitude can reduce the desire for unnecessary spending and increase contentment with your financial situation.
3. **Reflection:** Regularly reflect on your financial decisions and their impact on your goals. Use this reflection to learn from past

experiences and make more informed choices in the future.
4. **Set Intentions:** Set clear intentions for your financial goals and actions. Mindful intentions help you stay focused and motivated, even when faced with challenges.
5. **Stay Present:** Focus on the present moment and avoid dwelling on past financial mistakes or future uncertainties. Being present allows you to make thoughtful and deliberate financial decisions.
6. **Practice Self-Compassion:** Be kind to yourself and recognize that everyone makes financial mistakes. Practice self-compassion and use setbacks as opportunities for growth and learning.

By incorporating mindfulness into your financial practices, you can enhance your financial well-being and achieve greater satisfaction with your financial journey.

The Impact of Technology on Personal Finance

Technology has revolutionized personal finance, making it easier to manage money, invest, and plan for the future. This chapter will explore fintech innovations, the rise of cryptocurrency and blockchain, the future of digital banking, and strategies for protecting yourself from cyber financial threats.

Fintech Innovations: Apps and Tools for Managing Money

Financial technology (fintech) has introduced numerous apps and tools that simplify money management. These innovations provide greater accessibility, efficiency, and control over personal finances. Here are some popular fintech apps and tools:

- **Budgeting Apps:** Apps like Mint, YNAB (You Need A Budget), and PocketGuard help you track expenses, create budgets, and manage your finances efficiently.
- **Expense Tracking:** Tools like Expensify, Trail Wallet, and Money Lover allow you to

track and categorize expenses, making it easier to monitor your spending habits.
- **Investment Platforms:** Apps like Robinhood, Betterment, and Acorns provide easy access to stock trading, robo-advisory services, and micro-investing opportunities.
- **Money Transfer Services:** Services like PayPal, Wise (formerly TransferWise), and Venmo enable quick and cost-effective international and domestic money transfers.
- **Cryptocurrency Wallets:** Wallets like Coinbase, Binance, and Ledger allow you to securely store, send, and receive cryptocurrencies.
- **Credit Monitoring:** Apps like Credit Karma, Experian, and myFICO help you monitor your credit score, receive alerts for changes, and access credit reports.
- **Bill Management:** Tools like Prism and PocketSmith help you manage bills, track due dates, and avoid late payments.

By leveraging these fintech apps and tools, you can streamline your financial management, make informed decisions, and achieve your financial goals more effectively.

Cryptocurrency and Blockchain

Cryptocurrency and blockchain technology have emerged as significant innovations in the financial world. Here's an overview of their impact on personal finance:

Cryptocurrency

Cryptocurrencies are digital or virtual currencies that use cryptography for security. They operate on decentralized networks based on blockchain technology. Key benefits of cryptocurrencies include:

- **Decentralization:** Cryptocurrencies operate without a central authority, reducing the risk of government interference or manipulation.
- **Security:** Cryptographic security makes cryptocurrencies resistant to fraud and hacking.
- **Accessibility:** Cryptocurrencies provide financial access to individuals without access to traditional banking services.
- **Lower Transaction Fees:** Cryptocurrency transactions typically have lower fees compared to traditional banking and money transfer services.

Popular cryptocurrencies include Bitcoin (BTC), Ethereum (ETH), and Ripple (XRP). However, it's important to note that cryptocurrencies are highly volatile and can carry significant risks.

Blockchain Technology

Blockchain is the underlying technology behind cryptocurrencies. It is a distributed ledger that records transactions across multiple computers, ensuring transparency and security. Key applications of blockchain technology include:

- **Smart Contracts:** Self-executing contracts with the terms of the agreement directly written into code. Smart contracts automatically execute transactions when predefined conditions are met.
- **Supply Chain Management:** Blockchain can improve supply chain transparency, traceability, and efficiency by providing a secure and immutable record of transactions.
- **Decentralized Finance (DeFi):** DeFi platforms use blockchain to offer financial services like lending, borrowing, and trading without intermediaries. This increases accessibility and reduces costs.
- **Digital Identity:** Blockchain can provide secure and verifiable digital identities, reducing the risk of identity theft and fraud.

Blockchain technology has the potential to revolutionize various industries, including finance, healthcare, and supply chain management.

The Future of Digital Banking

Digital banking is rapidly evolving, driven by advancements in technology and changing consumer preferences. Here are some key trends shaping the future of digital banking:

Mobile Banking

Mobile banking apps provide convenient access to banking services, allowing customers to manage accounts, transfer money, pay bills, and more from their smartphones. The future of mobile banking includes enhanced user experiences, increased security features, and expanded services.

Open Banking

Open banking refers to the practice of sharing financial data between banks and third-party providers through APIs (Application Programming Interfaces). This promotes competition and innovation, leading to more personalized financial services and better customer experiences.

Artificial Intelligence and Machine Learning

AI and machine learning are transforming digital banking by enabling personalized financial advice, fraud detection, and predictive analytics. Chatbots and virtual assistants powered by AI provide instant customer support and streamline banking operations.

Biometric Authentication

Biometric authentication, such as fingerprint and facial recognition, enhances security and simplifies access to digital banking services. The adoption of biometrics is expected to increase, providing a more secure and seamless banking experience.

Neobanks

Neobanks are digital-only banks that offer a range of financial services without physical branches. They leverage technology to provide low-cost, user-friendly banking solutions. The rise of neobanks is disrupting traditional banking and expanding access to financial services.

Protecting Yourself from Cyber Financial Threats

As digital financial services become more prevalent, it's crucial to protect yourself from cyber financial threats. Here are some strategies to enhance your cybersecurity:

1. **Use Strong Passwords:** Create complex passwords for your financial accounts and change them regularly. Avoid using the same password for multiple accounts.
2. **Enable Two-Factor Authentication (2FA):** Use 2FA for an extra layer of security. This requires a second form of verification, such as a text message code, in addition to your password.
3. **Monitor Your Accounts:** Regularly check your bank and credit card statements for

unauthorized transactions. Report any suspicious activity immediately.
4. **Secure Your Devices:** Keep your devices updated with the latest security patches and antivirus software. Avoid using public Wi-Fi for financial transactions.
5. **Be Cautious with Emails and Links:** Beware of phishing emails and suspicious links. Verify the source before clicking on links or providing personal information.
6. **Use Secure Connections:** Ensure that the websites you use for financial transactions are secure (look for "https" in the URL). Avoid using financial apps on public or shared devices.
7. **Educate Yourself:** Stay informed about the latest cybersecurity threats and best practices. Knowledge is your best defense against cyber financial threats.

By implementing these strategies, you can protect your personal and financial information from cyber threats and enjoy the benefits of digital financial services securely.

Entrepreneurial Finance and Side Hustles

Starting a business or engaging in side hustles can be an excellent way to generate additional income and achieve financial independence. This chapter will explore strategies for funding your business, managing business finances, earning extra income through side hustles, and balancing personal and business finances.

Funding Your Business

Securing funding is a crucial step in launching and growing a business. Here are some common methods for funding your entrepreneurial ventures:

- **Personal Savings:** Using your savings to fund your business is a common approach. It allows you to maintain full control over your venture without taking on debt.
- **Bootstrapping:** Bootstrapping involves starting and growing your business with minimal external funding. This may include using personal resources, reinvesting profits, and keeping expenses low.
- **Friends and Family:** Borrowing money from friends and family can be a viable option. Ensure that you formalize the terms of the loan and communicate openly to avoid misunderstandings.

- **Bank Loans:** Traditional bank loans are a common source of funding for small businesses. They typically require a solid business plan and collateral.
- **Credit Cards:** Using credit cards can provide short-term financing. However, be cautious of high interest rates and ensure you have a plan to repay the balance quickly.
- **Angel Investors:** Angel investors are individuals who provide capital in exchange for equity in your business. They often offer valuable advice and mentorship in addition to funding.
- **Venture Capital:** Venture capital firms invest in startups with high growth potential in exchange for equity. This option is suitable for businesses looking to scale rapidly.
- **Crowdfunding:** Platforms like Kickstarter, Indiegogo, and GoFundMe allow you to raise funds from a large number of people, typically in exchange for rewards or equity.
- **Grants and Competitions:** Various organizations offer grants and business competitions that provide funding and resources for startups. Research opportunities in your industry and region.

Choosing the right funding method depends on your business model, financial needs, and long-term goals. Diversifying your funding sources can also help mitigate risk and ensure financial stability.

Managing Business Finances

Effective financial management is essential for the success of your business. Here are some tips for managing your business finances:

1. **Separate Personal and Business Finances:** Open a separate bank account for your business to keep your personal and business finances distinct. This simplifies accounting and helps you track business expenses accurately.
2. **Create a Budget:** Develop a detailed budget that outlines your business income and expenses. Regularly review and adjust your budget to ensure you stay on track and make informed financial decisions.
3. **Monitor Cash Flow:** Keep a close eye on your cash flow to ensure you have enough funds to cover operating expenses and unexpected costs. Implement cash flow management strategies, such as invoicing promptly and negotiating favorable payment terms with suppliers.
4. **Use Accounting Software:** Utilize accounting software like QuickBooks, Xero, or FreshBooks to automate bookkeeping tasks, generate financial reports, and track expenses. This helps you stay organized and maintain accurate records.
5. **Manage Debt Wisely:** If your business has debt, create a repayment plan to manage it effectively. Prioritize paying off high-interest

debt first and avoid taking on unnecessary debt.
6. **Plan for Taxes:** Understand your tax obligations and set aside funds to cover them. Consider working with a tax professional to ensure compliance and take advantage of available deductions and credits.
7. **Build an Emergency Fund:** Establish an emergency fund for your business to cover unexpected expenses or downturns in revenue. Aim to save at least three to six months' worth of operating expenses.

By implementing these financial management practices, you can ensure the long-term success and stability of your business.

Side Hustles: Earning Extra Income

Side hustles are a popular way to generate additional income and diversify your revenue streams. Here are some ideas for side hustles that can complement your primary income:

- **Freelancing:** Offer your skills and expertise as a freelancer in areas such as writing, graphic design, web development, consulting, or marketing. Platforms like Upwork, Fiverr, and Freelancer can help you find clients.
- **Online Selling:** Sell products online through platforms like Etsy, eBay, or Amazon. You

can create handmade items, source products from suppliers, or resell items for a profit.
- **Teaching and Tutoring:** Share your knowledge by offering online courses, tutoring, or coaching in subjects you are passionate about. Websites like Udemy, Teachable, and VIPKid provide opportunities for online teaching.
- **Content Creation:** Create content such as blogs, YouTube videos, or podcasts on topics that interest you. Monetize your content through ads, sponsorships, and affiliate marketing.
- **Gig Economy Jobs:** Participate in gig economy jobs like ridesharing (Uber, Lyft), food delivery (DoorDash, Uber Eats), or task-based services (TaskRabbit). These jobs offer flexible schedules and can be done alongside your main job.
- **Stock Photography:** If you have a talent for photography, sell your photos on stock photography websites like Shutterstock, Adobe Stock, or iStock.
- **Real Estate Rentals:** Rent out a spare room or property on platforms like Airbnb or Vrbo. This can generate significant income, especially if you live in a desirable location.

Side hustles not only provide extra income but also offer opportunities to explore your passions, develop new skills, and potentially turn a hobby into a profitable venture.

Balancing Personal and Business Finances

Balancing personal and business finances is essential for maintaining financial health and achieving your financial goals. Here are some tips to help you manage both effectively:

1. **Set Clear Boundaries:** Establish clear boundaries between your personal and business finances. Use separate bank accounts, credit cards, and accounting systems to avoid commingling funds.
2. **Pay Yourself a Salary:** Determine a reasonable salary for yourself based on your business income and personal financial needs. This helps you maintain a consistent income and budget for personal expenses.
3. **Track Personal and Business Expenses:** Regularly track and categorize your personal and business expenses. This helps you stay organized, manage cash flow, and ensure accurate financial records.
4. **Plan for Taxes:** Set aside funds for both personal and business taxes. Keep track of deductible expenses and consider working with a tax professional to optimize your tax strategy.
5. **Review Financial Goals:** Regularly review and update your personal and business financial goals. Ensure that your financial

plans align with your long-term objectives and make adjustments as needed.
6. **Monitor Financial Health:** Keep an eye on key financial metrics for both your personal and business finances. Monitor your savings rate, debt levels, cash flow, and investment performance to maintain financial health.
7. **Seek Professional Advice:** Consider working with financial advisors, accountants, or business consultants to receive personalized guidance and support. Professional advice can help you navigate complex financial decisions and achieve your goals.

By balancing personal and business finances effectively, you can ensure financial stability and success in all aspects of your life.

Philanthropy and Giving Back

Philanthropy and giving back are essential components of a fulfilling financial life. Contributing to the well-being of others not only makes a positive impact on society but also provides personal satisfaction and a sense of purpose. This chapter will explore the importance of philanthropy, strategies for effective giving, financial planning for charitable contributions, and the concepts of impact investing and social responsibility.

The Importance of Philanthropy

Philanthropy plays a vital role in addressing social issues, supporting communities, and fostering positive change. Here are some reasons why philanthropy is important:

- **Addressing Social Needs:** Philanthropic efforts help address critical social needs, such as poverty, education, healthcare, and environmental conservation.
- **Supporting Communities:** Charitable contributions strengthen communities by funding essential services, programs, and initiatives that benefit residents.
- **Promoting Equality:** Philanthropy can help reduce inequalities by providing resources and

opportunities to marginalized and underserved populations.
- **Enhancing Well-Being:** Giving back contributes to the overall well-being of society by improving quality of life, health outcomes, and access to education and resources.
- **Personal Fulfillment:** Engaging in philanthropic activities provides a sense of purpose and fulfillment, enhancing personal happiness and life satisfaction.

By embracing philanthropy, individuals can make a meaningful impact on the world and contribute to the greater good.

Strategies for Effective Giving

Effective giving involves thoughtful planning and consideration to maximize the impact of your charitable contributions. Here are some strategies to ensure your giving is effective and meaningful:

1. **Identify Your Values and Interests:** Reflect on your personal values and interests to determine the causes and organizations you are passionate about supporting.
2. **Research Organizations:** Conduct thorough research on charitable organizations to ensure they are reputable, transparent, and effective in achieving their mission. Look for organizations with a proven track record and strong financial health.

3. **Set Clear Goals:** Define clear goals for your philanthropic efforts. Consider what you hope to achieve and the impact you want to make with your contributions.
4. **Create a Giving Plan:** Develop a giving plan that outlines your charitable goals, budget, and preferred methods of giving. A structured plan helps you stay organized and committed to your philanthropic efforts.
5. **Consider Different Forms of Giving:** Explore various forms of giving, such as monetary donations, volunteer work, in-kind contributions, and fundraising efforts. Diversifying your giving methods can enhance your impact.
6. **Leverage Matching Gifts:** Take advantage of matching gift programs offered by employers or other organizations. Matching gifts can double or even triple the impact of your contributions.
7. **Evaluate Impact:** Regularly assess the impact of your charitable contributions. Review progress reports, outcomes, and feedback from the organizations you support to ensure your giving is making a meaningful difference.

By implementing these strategies, you can make your philanthropic efforts more effective and impactful.

Financial Planning for Charitable Contributions

Incorporating charitable contributions into your financial plan requires careful consideration and planning. Here are some tips for integrating philanthropy into your financial strategy:

1. **Budget for Giving:** Allocate a portion of your income or assets for charitable contributions. Establishing a giving budget ensures that philanthropy is a consistent and intentional part of your financial plan.
2. **Take Advantage of Tax Benefits:** Understand the tax benefits associated with charitable giving. Contributions to qualified charitable organizations may be tax-deductible, reducing your taxable income. Consider consulting with a tax professional to optimize your tax strategy.
3. **Use Donor-Advised Funds:** Donor-advised funds (DAFs) allow you to make a charitable contribution, receive an immediate tax deduction, and recommend grants to your chosen charities over time. DAFs provide flexibility and simplify the giving process.
4. **Consider Charitable Trusts:** Charitable remainder trusts (CRTs) and charitable lead trusts (CLTs) are estate planning tools that provide income to beneficiaries while benefiting charitable organizations. These

trusts offer tax advantages and can be part of a comprehensive giving strategy.
5. **Plan for Legacy Giving:** Include charitable bequests in your will or estate plan to ensure that your philanthropic values continue beyond your lifetime. Legacy giving allows you to make a lasting impact on the causes you care about.
6. **Engage with Financial Advisors:** Work with financial advisors who specialize in philanthropic planning. They can help you develop a giving strategy that aligns with your financial goals and values.

By integrating charitable contributions into your financial plan, you can support meaningful causes while achieving your financial objectives.

Impact Investing and Social Responsibility

Impact investing and social responsibility are approaches that align your financial decisions with your values. These strategies allow you to make a positive impact while generating financial returns. Here are some key concepts:

Impact Investing

Impact investing involves investing in companies, organizations, or funds with the intention of generating positive social or environmental impact alongside financial returns. Key considerations for impact investing include:

- **Identify Impact Goals:** Define your social or environmental impact goals. Consider the issues you are passionate about, such as renewable energy, affordable housing, or education.
- **Research Investment Opportunities:** Research impact investment opportunities that align with your goals. Look for funds, companies, or projects with a proven track record of positive impact and financial performance.
- **Evaluate Impact Metrics:** Assess the impact metrics used by investment opportunities to measure their social or environmental performance. Ensure that they use transparent and credible reporting practices.
- **Diversify Your Portfolio:** Diversify your impact investments across different sectors, asset classes, and geographies to manage risk and maximize impact.
- **Monitor Performance:** Regularly review the financial and impact performance of your investments. Stay informed about developments in the impact investing space and adjust your portfolio as needed.

Socially Responsible Investing (SRI)

Socially responsible investing (SRI) involves selecting investments based on ethical, social, and environmental criteria. SRI strategies include:

- **Negative Screening:** Excluding companies or industries that do not align with your values, such as tobacco, firearms, or fossil fuels.
- **Positive Screening:** Investing in companies that demonstrate strong environmental, social, and governance (ESG) practices.
- **Shareholder Advocacy:** Using your shareholder rights to influence corporate behavior and promote positive change through voting and engagement.
- **Community Investing:** Directing capital to underserved communities and projects that provide social benefits, such as affordable housing or small business development.

SRI allows you to align your investment portfolio with your values and contribute to positive social and environmental outcomes.

Financial Planning for Different Life Stages

Financial planning is a dynamic process that evolves as you progress through different stages of life. Each life stage presents unique financial challenges and opportunities. This chapter will explore financial planning strategies for young adults, mid-life individuals, and seniors, as well as tips for adapting your financial plan over time.

Financial Planning for Young Adults

Young adulthood is a critical time to establish a strong financial foundation. Here are key financial planning strategies for young adults:

1. **Create a Budget:** Develop a budget that tracks your income and expenses. A budget helps you manage your money effectively and avoid overspending.
2. **Build an Emergency Fund:** Aim to save at least three to six months' worth of living expenses in an easily accessible account. An emergency fund provides a financial cushion for unexpected expenses.
3. **Pay Off Debt:** Prioritize paying off high-interest debt, such as credit card balances and

student loans. Reducing debt frees up more money for saving and investing.
4. **Start Saving for Retirement:** Begin contributing to a retirement account, such as a 401(k) or IRA, as early as possible. Take advantage of employer matching contributions and the power of compound interest.
5. **Invest in Your Career:** Invest in education, training, and professional development to enhance your skills and increase your earning potential.
6. **Build Credit:** Establish and maintain good credit by paying bills on time, keeping credit card balances low, and monitoring your credit report regularly.

By implementing these strategies, young adults can build a solid financial foundation and set themselves up for long-term financial success.

Mid-Life Financial Strategies

Mid-life is a time to focus on building wealth, securing your financial future, and preparing for retirement. Here are key financial strategies for individuals in mid-life:

1. **Maximize Retirement Contributions:** Increase your contributions to retirement accounts, such as 401(k)s, IRAs, and HSAs. Aim to contribute the maximum allowed by tax laws.

2. **Review and Adjust Your Investment Portfolio:** Ensure your investment portfolio is diversified and aligned with your risk tolerance and financial goals. Rebalance your portfolio periodically to maintain the desired asset allocation.
3. **Plan for College Expenses:** If you have children, start saving for their education using tax-advantaged accounts like 529 plans or Coverdell ESAs.
4. **Pay Down Mortgage and Other Debts:** Focus on paying down your mortgage and other long-term debts. Reducing debt can provide financial flexibility and security.
5. **Build a Comprehensive Insurance Plan:** Ensure you have adequate health, life, disability, and long-term care insurance to protect your family and assets.
6. **Estate Planning:** Create or update your estate plan, including a will, power of attorney, and healthcare directive. Consider setting up trusts to manage and protect your assets.

By focusing on these strategies, mid-life individuals can strengthen their financial position and prepare for a secure retirement.

Financial Considerations for Seniors

Seniors need to focus on managing their retirement income, preserving wealth, and ensuring their financial affairs are in order. Here are key financial considerations for seniors:

1. **Manage Retirement Income:** Develop a retirement income plan that includes Social Security benefits, pensions, annuities, and withdrawals from retirement accounts. Ensure your income meets your living expenses.
2. **Minimize Taxes:** Use tax-efficient withdrawal strategies to minimize taxes on your retirement income. Consider consulting with a tax professional to optimize your tax situation.
3. **Protect Your Assets:** Protect your assets from potential risks by maintaining adequate insurance coverage and exploring long-term care insurance options.
4. **Estate Planning:** Review and update your estate plan to ensure your wishes are carried out. Consider creating a trust to manage your assets and provide for your heirs.
5. **Healthcare Planning:** Plan for healthcare expenses in retirement, including Medicare and supplemental insurance. Set aside funds for potential long-term care needs.
6. **Stay Engaged:** Stay engaged and active in your community and pursue hobbies and interests that bring you joy. Maintaining a healthy lifestyle can reduce healthcare costs and improve your quality of life.

By focusing on these considerations, seniors can enjoy a secure and fulfilling retirement.

Adapting Your Financial Plan Over Time

Your financial plan should evolve as your circumstances and goals change. Here are tips for adapting your financial plan over time:

1. **Review Your Plan Regularly:** Review your financial plan at least annually to ensure it remains aligned with your goals and circumstances. Make adjustments as needed.
2. **Set New Goals:** As you achieve your financial goals, set new ones to continue progressing. Consider short-term, medium-term, and long-term goals.
3. **Adjust for Life Changes:** Adapt your financial plan for significant life events, such as marriage, the birth of a child, job changes, or retirement. These events can impact your financial situation and goals.
4. **Stay Informed:** Stay informed about changes in tax laws, financial markets, and economic conditions that may affect your financial plan. Continuously educate yourself about personal finance and investing.
5. **Seek Professional Advice:** Consider working with financial advisors, accountants, or estate planners to receive personalized guidance and support. Professional advice can help you navigate complex financial decisions and achieve your goals.

By regularly reviewing and adapting your financial plan, you can stay on track to achieve your financial goals and maintain financial security throughout your life.

Global Perspectives on Personal Finance

Understanding personal finance from a global perspective can provide valuable insights and strategies for managing money effectively across different cultural and economic contexts. This chapter will explore comparing personal finance across cultures, managing finances as an expat, currency exchange and international investing, and the impact of global economic trends on personal finance.

Comparing Personal Finance Across Cultures

Personal finance practices can vary significantly across cultures due to differences in economic conditions, social norms, and government policies. Here are some key aspects of how personal finance differs across cultures:

- **Savings Rates:** Savings habits can vary widely. For example, Asian countries like China and Japan tend to have higher savings rates compared to Western countries. Cultural values emphasizing frugality and future security influence these habits.
- **Debt Attitudes:** Attitudes toward debt can differ. In some cultures, taking on debt is common and accepted, while in others, it is

avoided. For instance, credit card usage is prevalent in the United States, whereas many Germans prefer to use cash or debit cards.
- **Investment Preferences:** Investment strategies can be influenced by cultural attitudes toward risk. Americans often invest heavily in stocks, while Europeans may prefer real estate or government bonds.
- **Retirement Planning:** Retirement planning approaches can differ based on the availability of public pension systems. Countries with robust social security systems may see less emphasis on individual retirement savings compared to those with less generous public pensions.
- **Financial Education:** The level of financial literacy and education varies. Some countries prioritize financial education in schools, while others leave it to individuals to learn through experience.

By understanding these cultural differences, you can adapt your personal finance strategies to align with the practices and norms of the country you are in.

Managing Finances as an Expat

Living and working abroad as an expatriate (expat) presents unique financial challenges and opportunities. Here are some tips for managing your finances as an expat:

1. **Open Local Bank Accounts:** Open a local bank account in your host country to facilitate everyday transactions, receive your salary, and pay bills. Research banks that offer services tailored to expats.
2. **Understand Tax Obligations:** Familiarize yourself with the tax laws in both your home country and host country. Ensure you comply with tax filing requirements and take advantage of any tax treaties that may reduce double taxation.
3. **Create a Budget:** Develop a budget that accounts for the cost of living in your host country. Factor in expenses such as housing, transportation, healthcare, and leisure activities.
4. **Save for Emergencies:** Maintain an emergency fund in both your home and host countries. This provides a financial safety net in case of unexpected events or a sudden need to return home.
5. **Invest Wisely:** Consider diversifying your investments across multiple currencies and asset classes. Use investment platforms that offer access to global markets and low transaction fees.
6. **Health Insurance:** Ensure you have comprehensive health insurance coverage that meets your needs in your host country. Research local healthcare options and international health insurance plans.
7. **Stay Connected with Financial Advisors:** Maintain relationships with financial advisors

in both your home and host countries. They can provide valuable advice and help you navigate complex financial situations.

By taking these steps, you can effectively manage your finances and enjoy a secure financial future as an expat.

Currency Exchange and International Investing

Currency exchange and international investing are important aspects of managing finances globally. Here are some key considerations:

Currency Exchange

Managing currency exchange effectively can help you minimize costs and maximize the value of your money:

- **Use Multi-Currency Accounts:** Multi-currency accounts allow you to hold and manage funds in different currencies, reducing the need for frequent conversions.
- **Monitor Exchange Rates:** Keep an eye on exchange rates and convert currency when rates are favorable. Use currency exchange apps and websites to stay updated.
- **Avoid High Fees:** Use services that offer competitive exchange rates and low fees for currency conversions and international

transfers, such as Wise (formerly TransferWise) or Revolut.
- **Plan Ahead:** Plan your currency needs in advance to take advantage of favorable exchange rates and avoid last-minute conversions at unfavorable rates.

International Investing

Investing internationally can provide diversification and access to growth opportunities in different markets. Here are some tips for international investing:

- **Diversify Your Portfolio:** Spread your investments across various countries, industries, and asset classes to reduce risk and enhance potential returns.
- **Research Markets:** Conduct thorough research on the economic conditions, market trends, and political stability of the countries you are considering for investment.
- **Use International Brokers:** Work with brokers and investment platforms that offer access to global markets and provide tools and resources for international investing.
- **Understand Currency Risk:** Be aware of the potential impact of currency fluctuations on your investments. Consider using hedging strategies to manage currency risk.
- **Stay Informed:** Keep up-to-date with global economic developments, market news, and

geopolitical events that may affect your international investments.

By managing currency exchange effectively and investing internationally, you can enhance your financial strategy and achieve greater diversification and growth.

Global Economic Trends and Their Impact

Global economic trends can have a significant impact on personal finance. Understanding these trends can help you make informed financial decisions. Here are some key global economic trends to watch:

Economic Growth and Recession

Economic growth and recession cycles affect employment, income, and investment opportunities. Staying informed about global economic conditions can help you anticipate changes and adjust your financial strategy accordingly.

Inflation and Deflation

Inflation reduces the purchasing power of money, while deflation increases it. Monitor inflation rates in the countries where you live, work, or invest, and adjust your financial plan to protect against the adverse effects of inflation or deflation.

Interest Rates

Interest rates influence borrowing costs, savings returns, and investment performance. Keep an eye on central bank policies and global interest rate trends to make informed decisions about loans, savings, and investments.

Trade Policies and Globalization

Trade policies and globalization impact international trade, investment opportunities, and economic growth. Stay informed about trade agreements, tariffs, and global supply chain dynamics that may affect your financial interests.

Technological Advancements

Technological advancements drive innovation and economic growth but can also disrupt industries and job markets. Embrace new technologies that enhance personal finance management and stay adaptable to changes in the economic landscape.

Environmental and Social Issues

Environmental and social issues, such as climate change and social inequality, influence economic stability and investment opportunities. Consider incorporating environmental, social, and governance (ESG) criteria into your investment decisions.

By staying informed about global economic trends, you can make proactive and informed financial decisions that align with your goals and adapt to changing conditions.

Navigating Financial Resources and Tools

Access to the right financial resources and tools is essential for effective money management and informed decision-making. This chapter will explore valuable books, courses, and seminars for financial education, the benefits of utilizing financial advisors and planners, online resources and communities, and the importance of continuous learning and staying informed.

Books, Courses, and Seminars for Financial Education

Educating yourself about personal finance is the foundation for achieving financial success. Here are some recommended books, courses, and seminars to enhance your financial knowledge:

Books

- **"Rich Dad Poor Dad" by Robert T. Kiyosaki:** This classic book offers insights into the mindset and principles of building wealth and achieving financial independence.
- **"The Total Money Makeover" by Dave Ramsey:** Dave Ramsey provides a step-by-step guide to getting out of debt, building savings, and achieving financial peace.

- **"Your Money or Your Life" by Vicki Robin and Joe Dominguez:** This book explores the relationship between money and life satisfaction and offers a nine-step program for financial transformation.
- **"The Millionaire Next Door" by Thomas J. Stanley and William D. Danko:** Based on extensive research, this book reveals the habits and behaviors of America's wealthy individuals.
- **"The Intelligent Investor" by Benjamin Graham:** A classic investment book that provides timeless advice on value investing and building a solid investment strategy.

Courses

- **Financial Peace University:** Offered by Dave Ramsey, this course covers budgeting, saving, debt elimination, and wealth building through a series of video lessons and group discussions.
- **edX Personal Finance Courses:** edX offers a variety of free and paid courses on personal finance topics, including budgeting, investing, and retirement planning, from top universities.
- **Coursera Personal Finance Courses:** Coursera provides access to courses from leading institutions on topics such as financial planning, investment strategies, and financial literacy.
- **Udemy Personal Finance Courses:** Udemy offers a wide range of affordable courses on

personal finance, covering topics like financial independence, real estate investing, and stock market investing.

Seminars

- **Money Smart Week:** An annual public awareness campaign offering free seminars and workshops on various personal finance topics, organized by the Federal Reserve Bank of Chicago and partnering organizations.
- **Financial Planning Association (FPA) Events:** FPA hosts conferences, webinars, and workshops for financial professionals and consumers to learn about financial planning and industry trends.
- **Local Community Workshops:** Many community centers, libraries, and nonprofit organizations offer free or low-cost financial workshops on topics like budgeting, credit management, and retirement planning.

By leveraging these educational resources, you can build a strong foundation of financial knowledge and skills.

Utilizing Financial Advisors and Planners

Working with financial advisors and planners can provide personalized guidance and support for achieving your financial goals. Here are some benefits and tips for utilizing financial professionals:

Benefits of Financial Advisors and Planners

- **Expertise:** Financial advisors and planners have specialized knowledge and experience in areas such as investments, retirement planning, tax strategies, and estate planning.
- **Personalized Advice:** Advisors provide tailored recommendations based on your unique financial situation, goals, and risk tolerance.
- **Comprehensive Planning:** Financial planners take a holistic approach to your finances, considering all aspects of your financial life and creating an integrated plan.
- **Accountability:** Advisors help you stay on track with your financial goals by providing regular reviews, updates, and adjustments to your plan.
- **Stress Reduction:** Working with a professional can reduce financial stress and provide peace of mind, knowing that your finances are being managed effectively.

Tips for Choosing Financial Advisors and Planners

- **Check Credentials:** Look for advisors with reputable credentials, such as Certified

Financial Planner (CFP), Chartered Financial Analyst (CFA), or Certified Public Accountant (CPA).
- **Understand Fee Structures:** Financial advisors may charge fees based on assets under management (AUM), hourly rates, or flat fees. Ensure you understand their fee structure and how it aligns with your needs.
- **Research Background and Experience:** Investigate the advisor's background, experience, and areas of expertise. Look for reviews, testimonials, and references from current or past clients.
- **Assess Communication and Compatibility:** Choose an advisor who communicates clearly, listens to your concerns, and aligns with your values and financial goals.
- **Verify Fiduciary Status:** Ensure the advisor acts as a fiduciary, meaning they are legally obligated to act in your best interest.

By choosing the right financial advisor or planner, you can benefit from expert guidance and support in achieving your financial goals.

Online Resources and Communities

Online resources and communities offer valuable information, tools, and support for managing your finances. Here are some recommended online resources and communities:

Online Resources

- **Investopedia:** A comprehensive resource for financial education, offering articles, tutorials, and a financial dictionary covering a wide range of topics.
- **NerdWallet:** A personal finance website providing tools, calculators, and articles on budgeting, credit cards, loans, and investing.
- **The Balance:** A website offering practical advice on money management, investing, retirement planning, and more.
- **Mint:** A free budgeting tool and financial management app that helps you track expenses, create budgets, and monitor your financial health.
- **Morningstar:** A platform offering investment research, analysis, and tools to help you make informed investment decisions.

Online Communities

- **Reddit Personal Finance:** A popular online community where users share advice, ask questions, and discuss personal finance topics. Subreddits like r/personalfinance and r/financialindependence are valuable resources.
- **Bogleheads Forum:** A community of investors inspired by the principles of John Bogle, founder of Vanguard. The forum offers discussions on investing, retirement planning, and financial management.

- **Financial Independence Community:** Online forums and groups focused on achieving financial independence and early retirement (FIRE). These communities provide support, advice, and inspiration.
- **Facebook Groups:** Numerous Facebook groups are dedicated to personal finance, budgeting, investing, and financial independence. These groups offer a platform for sharing experiences and seeking advice.

By engaging with these online resources and communities, you can access valuable information, tools, and support for managing your finances effectively.

Continuous Learning and Staying Informed

Personal finance is a dynamic field that evolves with changes in economic conditions, tax laws, and financial products. Continuous learning and staying informed are crucial for effective financial management. Here are some tips for ongoing financial education:

1. **Read Financial News:** Stay updated on financial news and trends by reading reputable sources such as The Wall Street Journal, Bloomberg, and Financial Times.
2. **Follow Financial Blogs:** Follow personal finance blogs that provide insights, tips, and

updates on various financial topics. Some popular blogs include The Simple Dollar, Mr. Money Mustache, and The Penny Hoarder.
3. **Listen to Podcasts:** Podcasts offer an accessible way to learn about personal finance while on the go. Some recommended podcasts include "The Dave Ramsey Show," "ChooseFI," and "How to Money."
4. **Attend Webinars and Workshops:** Participate in webinars and workshops offered by financial institutions, non-profit organizations, and educational platforms. These events provide valuable information and networking opportunities.
5. **Join Professional Associations:** Join professional associations related to finance, such as the Financial Planning Association (FPA) or the National Association of Personal Financial Advisors (NAPFA). These organizations offer resources, events, and continuing education opportunities.
6. **Take Continuing Education Courses:** Enroll in continuing education courses on personal finance, investing, and financial planning through local colleges, universities, or online platforms.
7. **Network with Financial Professionals:** Build relationships with financial professionals and peers to exchange knowledge, share experiences, and stay informed about industry developments.

By committing to continuous learning and staying informed, you can adapt to changes in the financial landscape and make informed decisions that support your financial goals.

Your Financial Action Plan

Creating and implementing a personalized financial action plan is essential for achieving your financial goals. This chapter will guide you through the process of creating your financial plan, setting short-term and long-term goals, tracking progress, adjusting plans, and maintaining financial discipline and motivation.

Creating Your Personalized Financial Plan

Your financial plan serves as a roadmap for managing your money and achieving your financial goals. Here are the steps to create a personalized financial plan:

1. **Assess Your Current Financial Situation:** Start by evaluating your current financial status. List your assets (savings, investments, property) and liabilities (debts, loans). Determine your net worth and analyze your income and expenses to understand your cash flow.
2. **Define Your Financial Goals:** Clearly define your short-term, medium-term, and long-term financial goals. These goals should be specific, measurable, achievable, relevant, and time-bound (SMART).

3. **Create a Budget:** Develop a budget that aligns with your financial goals. Track your income and expenses, and allocate funds towards savings, investments, and debt repayment. Adjust your budget as needed to ensure it supports your goals.
4. **Establish an Emergency Fund:** Build an emergency fund with at least three to six months' worth of living expenses. This fund provides a financial cushion for unexpected expenses and emergencies.
5. **Develop a Debt Repayment Plan:** If you have outstanding debts, create a repayment plan. Prioritize paying off high-interest debt first and consider debt consolidation if it helps you manage your payments more effectively.
6. **Plan for Retirement:** Start saving for retirement as early as possible. Contribute to retirement accounts such as a 401(k), IRA, or Roth IRA, and take advantage of employer matching contributions.
7. **Invest Wisely:** Develop an investment strategy based on your risk tolerance and financial goals. Diversify your investments across different asset classes to manage risk and maximize returns.
8. **Protect Your Assets:** Ensure you have adequate insurance coverage for health, life, disability, and property. This protects your assets and provides financial security for you and your family.

By following these steps, you can create a comprehensive and personalized financial plan that serves as a foundation for achieving your financial goals.

Setting Short-Term and Long-Term Goals

Setting clear and achievable financial goals is crucial for maintaining focus and motivation. Here's how to set short-term and long-term financial goals:

Short-Term Goals

- **Emergency Fund:** Save enough money to cover three to six months' worth of living expenses.
- **Debt Reduction:** Pay off high-interest debt, such as credit card balances and personal loans, within a year.
- **Budget Management:** Create and stick to a monthly budget to track income and expenses.
- **Savings Targets:** Set specific savings targets for short-term needs, such as a vacation, home repairs, or a new car.

Long-Term Goals

- **Retirement Savings:** Accumulate enough savings and investments to support your desired lifestyle in retirement.
- **Home Ownership:** Save for a down payment and purchase a home.

- **Education Funding:** Save for your children's college education or your own further education.
- **Financial Independence:** Achieve financial independence by building a diversified investment portfolio that generates passive income.

By setting both short-term and long-term goals, you can create a balanced financial plan that addresses immediate needs and future aspirations.

Tracking Progress and Adjusting Plans

Regularly tracking your progress and adjusting your financial plan is essential for staying on course. Here are some tips for effective tracking and adjustment:

1. **Regular Reviews:** Review your financial plan and goals at least quarterly. Assess your progress and identify any areas that need adjustment.
2. **Use Financial Tools:** Utilize financial management tools and apps to track your income, expenses, savings, and investments. These tools can provide real-time insights and help you stay organized.
3. **Adjust Goals as Needed:** Life circumstances and financial goals can change over time. Be flexible and adjust your goals and plan as

needed to reflect your current situation and priorities.
4. **Celebrate Milestones:** Acknowledge and celebrate when you achieve your financial milestones. This helps maintain motivation and reinforces positive financial habits.
5. **Seek Professional Advice:** Consult with financial advisors or planners periodically to review your plan and make necessary adjustments. Professional advice can provide valuable insights and ensure you stay on track.

By consistently tracking your progress and making necessary adjustments, you can stay aligned with your financial goals and adapt to changing circumstances.

Maintaining Financial Discipline and Motivation

Maintaining financial discipline and motivation is key to achieving your financial goals. Here are some strategies to help you stay disciplined and motivated:

1. **Stay Focused on Your Goals:** Keep your financial goals at the forefront of your mind. Visualize the benefits of achieving your goals and remind yourself of the reasons behind them.
2. **Automate Savings and Investments:** Set up automatic transfers to your savings and investment accounts. Automation ensures consistency and reduces the temptation to spend.

3. **Create a Support System:** Share your financial goals with trusted friends or family members who can provide encouragement and accountability.
4. **Educate Yourself:** Continuously educate yourself about personal finance and investing. Staying informed helps you make better decisions and stay motivated.
5. **Practice Mindfulness:** Be mindful of your spending and financial decisions. Avoid impulsive purchases and focus on intentional, value-driven spending.
6. **Reward Yourself:** Allow yourself small rewards for achieving financial milestones. This reinforces positive behavior and keeps you motivated.
7. **Review and Reflect:** Regularly review your financial progress and reflect on your achievements. Celebrate your successes and learn from any setbacks.

By implementing these strategies, you can maintain financial discipline and motivation, ensuring steady progress toward your financial goals.

Conclusions

The journey to financial independence and stability is multifaceted, requiring a combination of knowledge, discipline, and strategic planning. Throughout this book, we have explored various aspects of personal finance tailored to the unique needs of digital nomads and individuals seeking financial freedom. As we conclude, let's revisit the key takeaways and principles that can guide you towards a secure and fulfilling financial future.

Key Takeaways

Each chapter of this book has provided valuable insights and practical strategies for managing different aspects of personal finance. Here are some of the key takeaways:

- **Understanding Financial Basics:** The foundation of financial success begins with understanding basic financial concepts such as budgeting, saving, investing, and debt management. These fundamental principles are crucial for making informed decisions and achieving your goals.
- **Embracing Technology:** Leveraging fintech innovations, online resources, and digital tools can streamline your financial management, making it easier to track expenses, invest, and plan for the future.

- **Investing Wisely:** Developing a diversified investment strategy aligned with your risk tolerance and financial goals is essential for growing your wealth and securing your future.
- **Planning for Retirement:** Early and consistent retirement planning, including saving in tax-advantaged accounts and understanding different retirement strategies, ensures a comfortable and secure retirement.
- **Managing Risks:** Protecting your assets and income through adequate insurance coverage, emergency funds, and risk management strategies helps safeguard your financial stability.
- **Adapting to Life Changes:** Financial planning is a dynamic process that requires regular review and adjustment to adapt to life changes, economic conditions, and evolving goals.
- **Global Perspective:** Understanding the global economic landscape, currency exchange, and international investing can provide new opportunities and insights for managing your finances.
- **Continuous Learning:** Staying informed and continuously educating yourself about personal finance, investing, and economic trends is crucial for making sound financial decisions.
- **Giving Back:** Philanthropy and social responsibility not only benefit society but also enrich your own life, providing a sense of purpose and fulfillment.

- **Creating a Financial Action Plan:** A well-crafted financial action plan, including setting short-term and long-term goals, tracking progress, and maintaining discipline, is essential for achieving financial success.

Final Thoughts

Achieving financial independence and stability is a lifelong journey that requires commitment, adaptability, and a proactive approach. By applying the principles and strategies discussed in this book, you can navigate the complexities of personal finance and work towards your financial goals with confidence.

Remember that financial success is not just about accumulating wealth but also about creating a life that aligns with your values, passions, and aspirations. Embrace the opportunities and challenges that come your way, and let your financial strategy support your adventurous and fulfilling life as a digital nomad.

Continuous Growth and Adaptation

The financial landscape is constantly evolving, influenced by technological advancements, economic shifts, and global trends. Stay adaptable and open to new ideas, continuously seeking opportunities for growth and improvement. By staying informed and proactive, you can make informed decisions that enhance your financial well-being and support your long-term goals.

Continuous growth also means being willing to learn from both successes and setbacks. Each financial decision, whether it results in gain or loss, offers valuable lessons that can inform your future strategies. Embrace these lessons and use them to refine your approach to personal finance.

Gratitude and Purpose

Finally, cultivate a mindset of gratitude and purpose in your financial journey. Recognize the progress you have made, celebrate your achievements, and remain focused on the positive impact you can have on your life and the lives of others. Whether through philanthropy, supporting loved ones, or contributing to your community, your financial success can create a ripple effect of positive change.

Gratitude helps maintain perspective and motivation, especially during challenging times. By acknowledging the resources and opportunities you have, you can foster a more positive and resilient approach to financial management.

Planning for the Future

As you plan for the future, consider not only your financial goals but also your personal aspirations and values. Financial planning is most effective when it aligns with your broader life goals. Reflect on what you want to achieve, both personally and financially, and let this guide your financial decisions.

Think about the legacy you want to leave, the experiences you want to have, and the impact you want to make. Your financial plan should be a tool that helps you realize these aspirations, providing the resources and security needed to pursue your dreams.

Building a Support System

Surround yourself with a support system that encourages and guides you on your financial journey. This can include financial advisors, mentors, family, friends, and like-minded individuals. A strong support network provides accountability, motivation, and diverse perspectives that can enhance your financial decision-making.

Engage with financial communities, whether online or in person, to share experiences, seek advice, and stay inspired. Collaborative learning and support can significantly enrich your financial journey.

Embracing Change and Innovation

Stay open to change and innovation in the financial world. Technological advancements, new financial products, and evolving economic conditions present both challenges and opportunities. Embrace these changes with a proactive mindset, continuously exploring how they can be leveraged to improve your financial strategy.

Innovation in financial technology (fintech) offers new tools and platforms that can simplify financial management, enhance investment strategies, and provide greater access to financial resources. Stay informed about these developments and consider integrating them into your financial plan where appropriate.

Credits

Published by entropunda in June 2024.

The cover has been designed using assets from Freepik.com.

Table of Contents

1. Mastering Personal Finance: Your Guide to Financial Independence
2. Introduction

Why Financial Independence Matters 202
What You'll Learn 202
Our Approach 202
Getting Started 202
Final Thoughts 202
Introduction to the Digital Nomad Lifestyle 202
Pros and Cons of Being a Digital Nomad 202
Financial Implications of a Nomadic Life 202
Setting Financial Goals for Digital Nomads 202
Creating a Budget: Tracking Income and Expenses 202
Building an Emergency Fund 202
Understanding Currency Exchange and Banking ... 202
Creating a Flexible Budget 202
Managing Variable Income 202
Building an Emergency Fund While Traveling 202
Saving on Travel and Accommodation 202
Tracking Your Expenses 202
Maximizing Savings Through Smart Spending 202
Leveraging Financial Tools and Apps 202
Building Wealth through Investing 202
Retirement Planning for Digital Nomads 202
Tax Planning and Compliance 202
The Role of Credit in Personal Finance 202
Credit Scores and Reports 202
Strategies for Building and Maintaining Good Credit 202
Managing Debt Responsibly 202

Avoiding Common Debt Traps 202
Credit and Debt in Different Countries 202
Financial Tools for Managing Credit and Debt 202
Real-Life Case Studies 202
Planning for Future Financial Goals 202
Introduction to Investing 202
Types of Investments 202
Risk Management and Diversification 202
Building an Investment Portfolio 202
Investing for Passive Income 202
Tax Considerations for Digital Nomads 202
Introduction to Real Estate Investment 202
Types of Real Estate Investments 202
Buying Your First Property 202
Managing Rental Properties 202
Real Estate Investment Strategies 202
Leveraging Real Estate to Build Wealth 202
Case Studies and Success Stories 202
Navigating Legal and Regulatory Challenges 202
The Importance of Early Retirement Planning 202
Types of Retirement Accounts 202
Strategies for Building a Retirement Nest Egg 202
Retirement Options in Different Countries 202
Case Studies and Success Stories 202
Planning for a Flexible Retirement 202
Tax Strategies for Retirement 202
Healthcare Planning for Retirement 202
Creating a Retirement Withdrawal Strategy 202
The Importance of Early Retirement Planning 202
Types of Retirement Accounts 202
Strategies for Building a Retirement Nest Egg 202
Retirement Options in Different Countries 202
Case Studies and Success Stories 202

Planning for a Flexible Retirement 202
Tax Strategies for Retirement 202
Healthcare Planning for Retirement 202
Creating a Retirement Withdrawal Strategy 202
Understanding Tax Residency 202
Double Taxation and Tax Treaties 202
Foreign Earned Income Exclusion (FEIE) 202
Foreign Tax Credit (FTC) 202
Tax-Advantaged Accounts 202
Strategies for Reducing Tax Liability 202
Staying Compliant with Tax Regulations 202
Case Studies and Success Stories 202
Creating a Tax Plan for Digital Nomads 202
Essential Insurance for Digital Nomads 202
Health Insurance for Digital Nomads 202
Travel Insurance for Peace of Mind 202
Life and Disability Insurance 202
Liability Insurance for Digital Nomads 202
Managing Risks as a Digital Nomad 202
Case Studies and Success Stories 202
Choosing the Right Insurance Coverage 202
Budgeting for Families 202
Saving for Education 202
Managing Healthcare and Insurance 202
Estate Planning 202
Balancing Work and Family Life 202
Case Studies and Success Stories 202
Choosing the Right Bank 202
Managing Currency Exchange 202
Utilizing Financial Tools and Apps 202
Setting Up a Home Base 202
Dealing with Financial Emergencies 202
Case Studies and Success Stories 202

- Understanding Credit Scores and Reports 202
- Strategies for Building Good Credit 202
- Managing Credit While Traveling 202
- Dealing with Credit Challenges 202
- Leveraging Credit for Financial Growth 202
- Case Studies and Success Stories 202
- Introduction to Investing 202
- Types of Investments 202
- Risk Management and Diversification 202
- Building an Investment Portfolio 202
- Investing for Passive Income 202
- Tax Considerations for Digital Nomads 202
- Case Studies and Success Stories 202
- Planning for Long-Term Financial Goals 202
- The Concept of Financial Independence 202
- Strategies for Accelerating Financial Freedom 202
- Case Studies of Financially Independent Individuals 202
- Maintaining Wealth and Financial Health 202
- Navigating Financial Crises 202
- Strategies for Handling Unexpected Expenses 202
- Rebuilding After Financial Setbacks 202
- Resources for Financial Assistance 202
- Understanding Your Financial Behavior 202
- Overcoming Psychological Barriers to Financial Success 202
- Building Healthy Money Habits 202
- Mindfulness and Financial Well-being 202
- Fintech Innovations: Apps and Tools for Managing Money 202
- Cryptocurrency and Blockchain 202
- The Future of Digital Banking 202
- Protecting Yourself from Cyber Financial Threats 202

Funding Your Business 202
Managing Business Finances...................................202
Side Hustles: Earning Extra Income.......................202
Balancing Personal and Business Finances............202
The Importance of Philanthropy.............................202
Strategies for Effective Giving................................202
Financial Planning for Charitable Contributions....202
Impact Investing and Social Responsibility 202
Financial Planning for Young Adults......................202
Mid-Life Financial Strategies..................................202
Financial Considerations for Seniors......................202
Adapting Your Financial Plan Over Time..............202
Comparing Personal Finance Across Cultures.......202
Managing Finances as an Expat 202
Currency Exchange and International Investing 202
Global Economic Trends and Their Impact 202
Books, Courses, and Seminars for Financial Education..202
Utilizing Financial Advisors and Planners 202
Online Resources and Communities.......................202
Continuous Learning and Staying Informed 202
Creating Your Personalized Financial Plan............202
Setting Short-Term and Long-Term Goals.............202
Tracking Progress and Adjusting Plans..................202
Maintaining Financial Discipline and Motivation..202
Key Takeaways..202
Final Thoughts...202
Continuous Growth and Adaptation 202
Gratitude and Purpose 202
Planning for the Future...202
Building a Support System 202
Embracing Change and Innovation 202
The Digital Nomad Lifestyle 1

1.

      2.
      3.
      4.
      5.
      6.
      7.
3. <u>The Digital Nomad Lifestyle</u>
      1.
      2.
      3.
      4.
      5.
      6.
      7.
4. <u>Budgeting and Saving on the Road</u>
      1.
      2.
      3.
      4.
      5.
      6.
      7.
      8.
      9.
      10.
5. <u>Understanding Credit and Debt</u>
      1.
      2.
      3.
      4.
      5.
      6.
      7.

8.
9.
6. Smart Investing Principles
    1.
    2.
    3.
    4.
    5.
    6.
7. Real Estate and Property Investment
    1.
    2.
    3.
    4.
    5.
    6.
    7.
    8.
8. Retirement Planning on the Move
    1.
    2.
    3.
    4.
    5.
    6.
    7.
    8.
    9.
    10.
    11.
    12.
    13.
    14.

            15.
            16.
            17.
            18.
9. <u>Tax Planning and Compliance</u>
            1.
            2.
            3.
            4.
            5.
            6.
            7.
            8.
            9.
10. <u>Insurance and Risk Management</u>
            1.
            2.
            3.
            4.
            5.
            6.
            7.
            8.
11. <u>Financial Planning for Families</u>
            1.
            2.
            3.
            4.
            5.
            6.
12. <u>Navigating Banking and Currency Issues</u>
            1.
            2.

    3.
    4.
    5.
    6.
13. Building and Maintaining Credit on the Road
    1.
    2.
    3.
    4.
    5.
    6.
14. Investing for Digital Nomads
    1.
    2.
    3.
    4.
    5.
    6.
    7.
    8.
15. Achieving Financial Independence
    1.
    2.
    3.
    4.
16. Dealing with Financial Challenges
    1.
    2.
    3.
    4.
17. Behavioral Finance and Money Psychology
    1.
    2.

   3.
   4.
18. <u>The Impact of Technology on Personal Finance</u>
   1.
   2.
   3.
   4.
19. <u>Entrepreneurial Finance and Side Hustles</u>
   1.
   2.
   3.
   4.
20. <u>Philanthropy and Giving Back</u>
   1.
   2.
   3.
   4.
21. <u>Financial Planning for Different Life Stages</u>
   1.
   2.
   3.
   4.
22. <u>Global Perspectives on Personal Finance</u>
   1.
   2.
   3.
   4.
23. <u>Navigating Financial Resources and Tools</u>
   1.
   2.
   3.
   4.

24. Your Financial Action Plan
    1.
    2.
    3.
    4.
25. Conclusions
    1.
    2.
    3.
    4.
    5.
    6.
    7.
26. Credits

www.ingramcontent.com/pod-product-compliance
Lightning Source LLC
Chambersburg PA
CBHW071452220526
45472CB00003B/772